D1707950

CRIMINAL JUSTICE

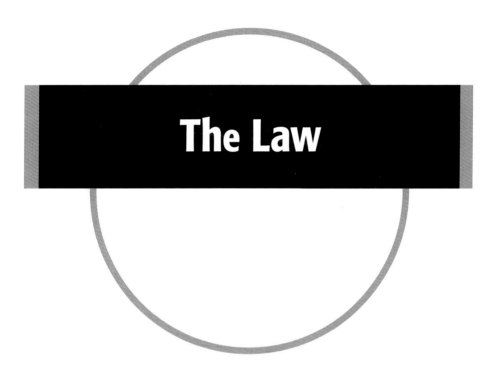

The Law

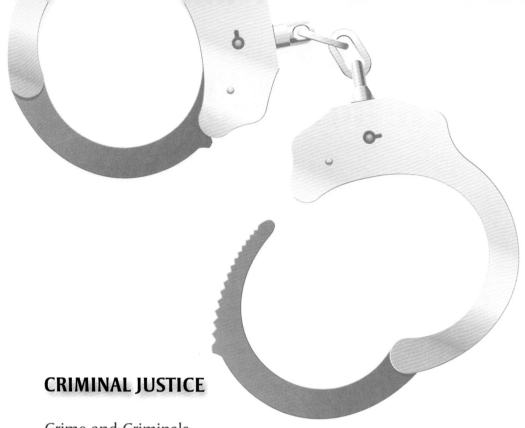

CRIMINAL JUSTICE

Crime and Criminals

Crime Fighting and Crime Prevention

Evidence

The Law

Prison and the Penal System

Trials and the Courts

CRIMINAL JUSTICE

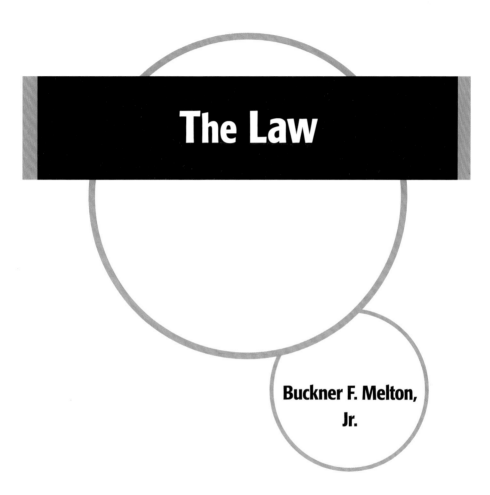

The Law

Buckner F. Melton, Jr.

CHELSEA HOUSE
PUBLISHERS

An imprint of Infobase Publishing

CRIMINAL JUSTICE: The Law

Chelsea House
An imprint of Infobase Publishing
132 West 31st Street
New York NY 10001

Library of Congress Cataloging-in-Publication Data
Melton, Buckner F.
The law / Buckner F. Melton, Jr.
p. cm. — (Criminal justice)
Includes bibliographical references and index.
ISBN-13: 978-1-60413-634-0 (hardcover : alk. paper)
ISBN-10: 1-60413-634-0 (hardcover : alk. paper) 1. Criminal law—United States—
Juvenile literature. 2. Criminal procedure—United States—Juvenile literature.
I. Title. II. Series.
KF9219.85.M45 2010
345.73—dc22

2009049081

Chelsea House books are available at special discounts when purchased
in bulk quantities for businesses, associations, institutions,
or sales promotions. Please call our Special Sales Department
in New York at (212) 967-8800 or (800) 322-8755.

You can find Chelsea House on the World Wide Web at http://www.chelseahouse.com

Text design by Erika K. Arroyo
Cover design by Keith Trego
Composition by EJB Publishing Services
Cover printed by Bang Printing, Brainerd, MN
Book printed and bound by Bang Printing, Brainerd, MN
Date printed: June 2010

Printed in the United States of America

10 9 8 7 6 5 4 3 2 1

This book is printed on acid-free paper.

All links and Web addresses were checked and verified to be correct at the time of
publication. Because of the dynamic nature of the Web, some addresses and links may
have changed since publication and may no longer be valid.

Contents

Acknowledgments

All of the subjects in this book deal with the relationship of crime to the legal process. But every one of these subjects is a major field of study in its own right. Each one of the eight chapters is typically the focus of a separate college or law school course lasting a quarter, a semester, or even a year, and many sections within chapters have been the subject of specialized volumes—and sometimes many such volumes.

Because of the wide range of materials in these pages, as well as the difficulty in condensing such a vast amount of subject matter into so short a book, I have sought feedback from readers of different ages and specialists in several fields. I am grateful for the input and assistance of Vicki Arnold, Gloria Boy, Christine Duryea, Katherine Duryea, Rachel Duryea, Marc Ermine, Deepa Gopalakrishnan, Jason Levitt, Christine Rodriguez, Matthew Rodriguez, Theresa Rodriguez, Grady Singleton, and Leigh Singleton. I am especially grateful to my agent, Ed Knappman, and (as always) to Dr. Carol K. Melton, aka "the power behind the drone."

I wish to dedicate this volume to my homeschool students who helped with the preparation of this book. Keep on learning!

Buckner F. Melton, Jr.
July 3, 2009

Introduction

Twenty-three centuries ago, the Greek philosopher Aristotle wrote that "man is by nature a political animal." By this, he meant that human beings naturally form and live in society with each other. Society, according to Aristotle, allows humanity to be secure and productive. On the other hand, he declared, without law and justice, people are at their worst, because they can then threaten the stability and peace of other members of society.

The law, then, exists to provide people with rules for living peacefully with each other. The criminal law, in particular, is concerned with the safety and protection of the society as a whole from dangerous actions by individuals in that society. A person who engages in criminal conduct can cause injury and death to fellow citizens, as well as great damage to valuable property. The criminal law is designed to reduce this danger by punishing those who engage in such conduct and by threatening to punish those who might be thinking about engaging in it.

The speed limit, for instance, is designed to protect not only the driver who might hurt or kill him or herself by driving too fast. It also protects other drivers or pedestrians he might run into; the insurance companies who would have to pay for any damage he or she causes; and the taxpayers whose money is needed to provide safe roads, ambulances, and fire and police departments, all of which might be involved in preventing or responding to a traffic accident. Theoretically, at least, when someone commits a crime, the entire society may suffer harmful effects. The criminal law is designed to protect society from these effects.

The criminal law is more than just a set of rules about things that people cannot do. It is also about how society applies those rules. If a police officer gives speeding tickets to men but not women, or to blacks but not to Latinos or whites—in other words, if he or she does not enforce the laws fairly—this will probably lead many or most members of society to see the law as unfair and to refuse to follow the law at all. If the government keeps a law secret from citizens until they actually break it or uses force or threats to wring a confession from someone accused (perhaps wrongly) of breaking the law, it would undermine the whole purpose of the criminal law as Western society understands it. So the criminal law must also have rules for how to go about investigating and punishing crimes to ensure that these processes are fair, and to make sure that persons who have engaged in criminal conduct—and no one else—are held accountable for that conduct.

In a republican society, one way of making sure that criminal laws are fair is to enact them through a democratic, legislative process, so that all of society may decide what conduct is criminal. Another way of safeguarding citizens from unfair uses of the criminal process is to write protections into the most fundamental law of the country (in the United States, the national and state constitutions). Still another way is to place the criminal law system under the supervision of courts, which in turn ensure that not only those who are accused of crime, but that the police and other government agencies, obey these fundamental protections and the criminal law generally.

Yet another way of making sure that the criminal law is fair is to give special treatment to people in special circumstances. One of the best examples of this is how the criminal law treats children; even though they may cause great damage if they behave in a criminal way, they also may be too young to appreciate the destructiveness of their behavior. As a result, special courts with special rules are usually involved in dealing with youth crime.

The criminal law, then, consists of many different areas. This book explores all of the above topics: the legal processes for investigating crime and for deciding the guilt or innocence of someone accused of committing a crime, the democratic system for deciding exactly what conduct amounts to a crime, and the nature of the court system used to decide criminal cases, including juvenile courts. Its opening chapters also examine some even more basic issues, including the question of why the law punishes criminal conduct to begin with, and the centuries-long history of criminal law systems.

Chapter 1, "The Nature of Criminal Law," looks at what sorts of actions are considered criminal and why.

Chapter 2, "The History of the Criminal Law," explores the evolution of law in western society and identifies landmark documents and principles that shape how criminal law is enacted and enforced today.

Chapter 3, "The Criminal Law and the American Federal System," discusses the ins and outs of how laws are created and passed in the United States, where laws may differ from state to state and between states and the federal government.

"The Process of Legislation," Chapter 4, explains how laws are passed and traces the path of a proposed law as legislators debate, amend, and vote on new laws.

"The Elements of Criminal Law," Chapter 5, breaks down the key principles of how criminal acts as well as guilt are defined by the law and how those definitions apply to criminal cases.

Chapter 6, "Criminal Procedure: Investigating the Crime," covers how criminal law shapes police investigations and what legal principles guide how law enforcement officials can collect and process evidence and question suspects.

Chapter 7, "Criminal Procedure: The Trial," explains how criminal cases are tried in court. It describes the foundations of the legal system, courtroom procedures, and how the law applies inside the courtroom during a criminal trial.

"The Juvenile Court System," Chapter 8, details the differences in how the law and the justice system treat minors. Because children may be incapable of fully understanding the consequences of their actions, a separate branch of law exists to govern them.

By reading this book thoroughly, the student can gain a good understanding of one of the most important topics involved in the safe and stable functioning of society: the criminal law.

The Nature of
Criminal Law

In 1884, a grisly event took place far out on the Atlantic. It was to become a notorious tale of the sea, as well as the basis for the most famous case in English and American **criminal law**.

In the 1880s, the sport of yachting was at a high point, as well-to-do English owners raced their prized vessels against each other. A wealthy Australian, wanting to share in the excitement, traveled to England to buy one of these yachts. He found one named the *Mignonette*, and he hired an experienced captain to sail her to Australia.

This captain, Thomas Dudley, took on a crew of three for the voyage: Edwin Stephens, the mate; sailor Edmund Brooks; and 17-year-old Richard Parker, who would serve as cabin boy. Unlike the others, Parker had never before gone to sea, but he wanted to see the world, and sailing to Australia seemed a good way to do so. In May 1884, *Mignonette* and her crew set forth on their 14,000-mile voyage.[1]

Yachts, being fairly small vessels, rarely make deep-sea voyages, and 47 days into her journey, as she traveled deep into the South Atlantic, *Mignonette* ran into trouble. The Southern hemisphere was in the middle of winter, and the yacht was forced to battle roaring gales and mountainous swells. On July 5 the worst happened. A towering wave swamped *Mignonette* and sank her in a matter of minutes.

As the vessel began to go down, the crew barely had time to lower the yacht's dinghy into the water and throw in a few tins of supplies.

Pulling away from the sinking *Mignonette*, they found that they had no fresh drinking water and only two small tins of turnips. The nearest land was hundreds of miles away. Their situation was desperate, and soon it would grow even worse.[2]

For the next two weeks, exposed to sun, wind, cold, and salt spray, the castaways hung on grimly. In all this time they spotted no ships and collected practically no rain water. A few days after the *Mignonette*'s loss, they managed to catch and eat a small turtle. But it wasn't nearly enough, and by July 20, all of them were dying of starvation and thirst.

Richard Parker was in the worst shape. Overcome by thirst, he had resorted to drinking seawater. But the ocean's salt actually dehydrated him even further, causing severe diarrhea and making him delirious. Soon he lay in the dinghy's bottom, scarcely able to move and almost unconscious.

It was around this time when Dudley mentioned a gruesome idea. It might be best, he suggested, if one of the boat's inhabitants be sacrificed to save the lives of the other three—by becoming a source of food.

Exactly what happened next is not entirely clear. The castaways were in bad condition both physically and mentally, and their memories afterward were poor. And even if they had remembered things well, they would not normally have wished to dwell on what had happened, or to talk about it too much. The survivors did vaguely mention the possibility of drawing straws to see who would be sacrificed, but no one knows whether they actually did. Brooks apparently disagreed with the whole idea of killing someone. And straws or not, Dudley and Stephens seemed to believe that Parker was the logical choice. He was the closest to death, and unlike the others he had no wife or children whom he had to support.

But a few things are very clear. Around July 24, give or take a day or two, Dudley made up his mind. Picking up his knife and saying a prayer in which he asked for forgiveness, he told Parker that the time had come, and then he cut the cabin boy's throat.[3]

A few days later, the German cargo ship *Moctezuma* sighted the dinghy and rescued Dudley, Stephens, and Brooks. The castaways made no secret of what they had done. It was tragic, but they were certain that Parker's death had saved their lives. And it was a fact that this sort of

Captain Thomas Dudley and mate Edward Stephens were later tried for the murder of Richard Parker, whom they sacrificed for the sake of their own survival. *Rischgitz/Getty Images*

thing had happened before. Sailors even had a name for cannibalism among castaways: They called it "the custom of the sea."

Moctezuma sailed to the seaport of Falmouth in England, where the castaways went ashore. Soon the townspeople learned what had happened, and so did the town constable. In light of what he learned from talking to Dudley and the others, he decided he had no choice but to arrest the three survivors for **murder**.

The case of Dudley and Stephens soon drew great attention. Brooks was not prosecuted. His claim that he had disapproved of the killing (even though he too had consumed some of Parker's remains), together with the **prosecutor**'s need for a witness against the others, saved him. But Dudley and Stephens were surprised, even shocked, to find themselves on **trial**. Most of Falmouth's residents believed that what they had done was understandable. Even Richard Parker's brother, Daniel, traveled to Falmouth to meet and talk with the three survivors and apparently did not blame them.[4] But to the prosecutors the law was clear. Dudley, with Stephens's agreement, had deliberately taken an innocent human life.

Both before and during the trial, Dudley and Stephens freely admitted what they had done. But they claimed that they had had to do it. If they hadn't killed Parker, their attorneys argued, everyone on the boat would probably have died before they were rescued. Surely one death was better than four.

The jury, refusing to decide the question of Dudley's and Stephens's guilt, referred the question to a panel of senior judges. It was a highly unusual move, but then this was an unusual case. It strongly resembled an ethical question that philosophers had debated for thousands of years. As early as 44 B.C., the Roman statesman Cicero had set forth the problem of two shipwrecked sailors holding onto a plank that could support only one of them. In that situation, Cicero had asked, would either of the men be justified in pushing the other one off the plank in order to save his own life?[5] Thinkers throughout the ages had raised the question again and again. Now the case of Dudley and Stephens asked it for real.

Legally the answer seemed clear, at least at first. Dudley and Stephens had deliberately, with premeditation, killed an innocent young man who was not threatening them with any danger. They claimed that the killing was necessary for them to survive, a claim that is known, for obvious reasons, as the defense of **necessity**. It was true that the law allows someone to kill another in **self-defense**. But that sort of killing, the *Dudley* court noted, is only justifiable when the killer is himself threatened with death or serious injury by the person he kills, and only when that threat is immediate—not days or hours away, but a matter of moments. None of this was the case here. Parker had threatened no one, and anyway he had had just as much right to live as Dudley, Stephens, and Brooks. And it was not even certain that the men would have died before the rescue unless they had killed Parker, since they sighted *Moctezuma* only a few days afterward. Because of all this, decided the court, the defense of necessity did not apply here.

The judges also noted that the right to survive, which Dudley and Stephens claimed, is not absolute. In war, for instance, a soldier's duty might be not to live but to die, to sacrifice his life for his comrades or for his nation. And any right that Dudley, Stephens, and Brooks did have to survive was a right that Parker had had as well. In light of this, the court ruled that it could not choose who in the boat deserved to live or die. The law was clear, and the fact was that Dudley and Stephens had broken that law. They were guilty of murder.

The punishment was also clear. In English murder cases at the time, judges had no discretion; a defendant convicted of murder was automatically sentenced to death. On December 9, therefore, Lord Coleridge, the senior judge in the case, pronounced the sentence: that Dudley and Stephens "be taken to the prison where you came, and that, on a day appointed for the purpose of your execution you be there hanged by the neck until you be dead."[6]

Today, law students throughout the English-speaking world regularly study the case of Dudley and Stephens. It is a case that raises several basic questions about the nature and purpose of the criminal law. Many of these questions are hard to answer, even after all these years. The questions also help to clarify many other aspects of the criminal law system. For that reason, they are good questions to keep in mind when reading this book. The following issues are some of the most important ones involved in the case of Dudley and Stephens.

THE RELATIONSHIP OF CRIME AND CRIMINALS TO SOCIETY

Criminal law can be defined as *a body of law that seeks to prevent harm to society by punishing certain types of conduct.* The *Dudley* case invites examination of that definition, specifically the relationship of criminals and their conduct to society at large.

Although Dudley, Stephens, Brooks, and Parker were all English subjects, they were thousands of miles from England and far from all other societies when Dudley killed Parker. They were cut off from any interaction with the rest of the human race. But upon their return to England—which, at the time of Parker's death, was something not at all sure to happen—English law treated the survivors as if they had been part of English society all along and therefore subject to its rules. But the conditions as well as the rules for surviving in an open boat far at sea seem to be quite different from conditions in England. In a situation such as this, should the law have treated the boat's occupants as if they were part of English society? Or instead should it have found that they made up their own independent community, with both the need and the right to make special rules for themselves?

Suppose, for a moment, that the court *had* found the boat to form an independent society that had rules of its own. (This legal game of "let's pretend" is called a *hypothetical question*, which is a very useful tool for analyzing the law.) How far should it have taken this idea? If a group of coal miners within the borders of England were trapped and cut off by a cave-in, then shouldn't the court view them, too, as a separate society with the right to practice cannibalism? What about the passengers and crew of an airplane flying over England? Aren't they, too, cut off from the rest of the world? Does this make them free to deal with a terrorist in any way they see fit without answering to the law of England once they land? What about passengers in a train, or a driver in a car who must deal with an unruly hitchhiker? What about a family in a remote house that must deal with a member who suddenly becomes violent? How isolated must the house be? Must it be isolated at all? In other words, once the idea that a group of people cut off from society are not answerable to that society is established, how far should that rule extend—and why should it extend exactly that far, not more and not less?[7]

THE RELATIONSHIP OF THE CRIMINAL LAW TO MORALITY

Morality involves fundamental questions of right and wrong, good and evil. Some of the most basic sources of morality are found within religions, systems of philosophy, and peoples' own consciences. Some would argue that law itself is another source of morality, or that every law has a moral basis. But even if this is so, immoral conduct is not always criminal, and criminal conduct is not always accepted as immoral. This difference is one of the things that makes the *Dudley* case such a difficult one.

The criminal law tries to prevent social harm. Its normal way of doing this is to prohibit bad conduct and to punish those who engage in it. Only rarely does the law work in the opposite way, by requiring good conduct and rewarding people who engage in it. To put this another way, the law is likely to punish Patricia if she drowns Carlos, but it does not usually reward Chris if she rescues Bob from drowning. (Bob himself may reward Chris, but that has nothing to do with criminal law.) It may be immoral for Chris to stand on the beach and watch Bob drown without trying to save him, especially if Chris is a champion swimmer, but it is not illegal. On the other hand, breaking the speed limit is illegal, but in certain situations it would not seem to be immoral, as when a husband is racing his wife to the hospital when she is in labor or needs emergency medical treatment.

HYPOTHETICAL QUESTIONS

In biology, chemistry, and physics, scientists can repeat the same experiment several times, while changing only a single variable. If the result changes from experiment to experiment as the scientist changes the variable, the different result must be due to the change in the variable. But in real-world episodes (such as crimes) involving different people and circumstances, events cannot be perfectly repeated, and they usually cannot be repeated at all. So lawyers and judges often *pretend* to repeat the events, while pretending to change a single fact, the way a scientist in the laboratory actually changes one variable. The lawyer then asks himself or others whether that one difference would, or should, make the legal result of the case different. By doing this, the lawyer can figure out whether, and why, some conduct is considered to be criminal and other conduct is not. The question is known as a hypothetical question. *Hypothetical* comes from a Greek word meaning "to suppose." Hypothetical questions are very important in legal analysis. In later chapters this book will use many hypothetical questions to help analyze the law.

Even the judges in the *Dudley* case recognized that law and morality are not always the same thing, and that the temptations of hunger and thirst faced by the boat's occupants must have been superhuman. Nevertheless, the court declared that judges "are often compelled to set up standards we cannot reach ourselves, and to lay down rules which we could not ourselves satisfy." But what forces judges to do this? And why did the judges see Parker's killing as not merely criminal but immoral as well?

The morality underlying the court's decision is that human life has an absolute value. Parker was an innocent human being with as much right to life as Dudley, Stephens, and Brooks. Because this was the case, then, Dudley had no right to kill Parker, who was not threatening Dudley. But is this view correct? Should it make a difference that Parker was very ill and likely to die soon? If so, why? If not, why not? On the one hand, we could say that if Parker were about to die anyway, then Dudley took very little from him by killing him. Perhaps Dudley even did Parker a favor by sparing him a day or two of suffering. And if human life has value, then killing one person to save the lives of three is an improvement over the deaths of all four, at least in numerical terms.

On the other hand, we could also argue that the law should most strongly protect exactly those people who are least able to protect themselves, such as the weak and the sick (in other words, people like Parker). It is also possible that Parker's life was even more valuable than usual because so little of it remained. And we must keep in mind that nobody in the boat or on the court knew for certain if Parker were actually about to die, or how much longer Dudley and the others could have gone without food. After all, they were rescued only a few days after they killed Parker. Perhaps the cabin boy's death wasn't necessary after all.

This was a case, then, in which the law was both clear and rigid, but the morality of applying that law to this case was not clear at all. This is one of the main reasons why many people believe that something is wrong about the outcome of the *Dudley* case. Another reason for this belief is involved with the issue of punishment.

THE DIFFERENT REASONS FOR CRIMINAL PUNISHMENT

The criminal law seeks to protect society from harm by punishing those who engage in criminal conduct. In fact, the idea of punishment is one of the most basic elements of the criminal law. But how, exactly, does punishment protect society? There are many possible answers, but none of them seems to apply in the *Dudley* case.

Incapacitation

One of the most straightforward reasons for punishing a criminal is to make sure that he never engages in criminal conduct again. This is known as incapacitation, because it takes away a criminal's capacity, or ability, to commit crimes. Execution of the criminal—that is, carrying out a sentence of death—is certainly a guaranteed way to do this. Imprisonment is also effective, but not to the same extent, since the incapacitation ends when the criminal is released (or escapes) from jail.

But in the *Dudley* case, was execution necessary? Did Dudley and Stephens need to be incapacitated in order to prevent them from committing cannibalism in the future? After all, they had been reluctant cannibals, resorting to their actions (as the court itself noted) only after maddening hunger and thirst. The likelihood that they would ever find themselves in such circumstances again, even in a dozen lifetimes, must have been extremely small. Why, then, should the law bother with incapacitating them?

Deterrence

A related goal of punishment is to deter, or discourage, people from engaging in criminal conduct in the future. On the one hand, punishment of Dudley and Stephens could be seen as discouraging *them* from committing further acts of cannibalism upon their release by teaching them that future cannibalism would lead to further punishment. This is known as *specific deterrence* since it is aimed specifically at the criminals themselves. On the other hand, punishment of Dudley and Stephens could serve as a warning to *other* members of society that if they were to commit cannibalism, they would receive the same punishment that Dudley and Stephens had. This approach is known as *general deterrence* because it is aimed at the general public. Of course, punishment of Dudley and Stephens could serve simultaneously as both specific and general deterrence.

As is the case with the incapacitation theory, the idea of deterrence seems not to apply in this case. Suppose, incredibly, that Dudley and

Stephens, after their release from prison, *did* someday find themselves adrift at sea once again with a third person and no food. Facing death by starvation within the next few hours or days, would they be deterred from committing a new act of cannibalism by the possibility that they might survive long enough to face another trial someday for murder? Almost certainly not. And the answer would be the same for any other member of society in the same circumstances.

In other words, the law can do little, if anything, to deter anyone from killing when he or she believes that he or she is facing death in the immediate future. Even the threat of execution is no deterrent, for nearly everyone would find that a possible execution months or years in the future is preferable to an apparently certain death within minutes or seconds (or in Dudley's and Stephens's case, hours or days). Because of this, the deterrent value of punishing Dudley and Stephens was probably nonexistent.

Reform/Education

A widespread, and controversial, theory of punishment is that of reform, or rehabilitation. This is not technically punishment, although like punishment it normally involves fines and imprisonment. Instead, it is an effort to find out why the criminal engaged in criminal conduct and to help him or her recognize and avoid the elements and behaviors in his or her life that caused him or her to break the law. Rehabilitation might also involve helping the criminal recognize that his or her conduct was socially unacceptable and that he or she should behave in more correct and positive ways in the future. The reform idea might even extend so far as to teach the criminal a more socially useful trade while he or she is in prison so that he or she will become a more valuable member of society upon his or her release. It is largely because of the reform theory that many American prison systems are called "departments of corrections."

But this theory, too, fails to fit the *Dudley* case. Neither Dudley nor Stephens needed to be reformed or taught that their actions had been wrong. Dudley, after all, had said a prayer asking forgiveness just moments before killing Parker. This clearly shows that Dudley was contemplating an action that he at least knew to be immoral, if not criminal. Stephens, for his part, could not even bring himself to help Dudley kill Parker.

As for learning a useful trade, Dudley had been a sailor since the age of nine. He had served as sailing master and mate on several ships, and he held a mate's certificate from the Board of Trade. Stephens, for his part, was certified as a Master Mariner—a very high level of achievement among sailors. In short, the two men were already valuable members of society at the time of Parker's death. So any attempt at reforming them was pointless, since they were skilled contributors to their society who knew that they were engaging in wrongdoing even at the time they did it.

Retribution

The final, and oldest, reason for punishing is retribution, or vengeance—the idea of getting back at someone for his criminal conduct, or, in common terms, "payback" or "just deserts." At the most primitive level, Richard Parker's family would have been the ones to seek revenge by killing Dudley and Stephens, since the family is the most basic building block of society and Parker's death would likely have had the greatest financial and emotional impact on his relatives. In more modern societies, the law itself, acting through the government, is the one to take this kind of vengeance.

Retribution is a theory that has serious problems. For one thing, Richard Parker's brother Daniel had already met with Dudley and Stephens before the trial, shaking their hands and apparently forgiving them, or at least accepting on some level what they had done. If the family, as represented by Daniel, had taken this approach, then why should society involve itself and override Daniel's judgment? Furthermore, Dudley and Stephens killed only one person. In light of this, would it be fair to punish two people—both Dudley and Stephens—in exchange? If the families of Dudley and Stephens thought not, then would that justify another round of revenge killing—perhaps of the hangman or even the judge—to even out the numbers? After all, if it was wrong for a small group—Dudley and Stephens—to kill Parker, then wouldn't it be equally wrong for a larger group—society—to take a life, especially if it took more lives than it should have in order to even the score? In short, if taking life is wrong, then isn't it wrong for everyone? And if so, then the old saying that "two wrongs don't make a right" must be considered.

On the other hand, suppose it is all right for society at large to take a life through the criminal process. Why should this be so? This goes back to the starting point: the relationship of a society safely on land to the small group in the boat thousands of miles at sea. Why should that society's rules apply to Dudley and Stephens? Who can say that society was right and that they were wrong?

After the court sentenced the two men to death, their story entered its final strange chapter. Most of the public, as well as many government officials, believed that, given the facts of the case, a death sentence was too harsh a punishment. The judges themselves even mentioned the possibility of a pardon, even though they themselves were bound by the law to find the prisoners guilty and to sentence them to hang. And several days later, on the recommendation of her advisors, Queen Victoria reduced the sentence to six months in prison, clearly because she and her officials believed that this was the best way to achieve justice in the *Dudley* case.

THE RELATIONSHIP BETWEEN LAW AND JUSTICE

This outcome raises a final series of important questions about the relationship between law and justice. The word "law" has several meanings, but one of the most basic ideas behind it is that of a rule, or a system of rules, that applies to everyone, or at least to everyone within a certain category. Traffic signals, for instance, normally must be obeyed by all drivers. The law, in other words, seeks to treat like persons in like fashion.

Justice, on the other hand, involves treating each person the way he or she deserves to be treated based on his or her particular circumstances. In a sense, then, justice is the opposite of law: Since everyone's circumstances are different from everyone else's, in a system of perfect justice there could be no rules—no laws. But such a society would quickly become chaotic. What if every driver were free to drive based on his or her particular reflexes, attention span, vision, ability to afford a faster or slower car, and need to arrive at work in time for an important meeting? Traffic would likely become chaotic and extremely dangerous (as if it weren't dangerous enough already).

Oliver Wendell Holmes, Jr., Justice of the U.S. Supreme Court, sits in his home in March 1931. *AP Photo*

Another problem with justice is how a society would decide what someone deserves. This usually involves an appeal to the judge's (or in the case of Dudley and Stephens, the Queen's) conscience, or to morality, or to an ethical system, or even to public opinion. Different people may have different views on matters of conscience or morals or the important facts of the case. So justice is a difficult and at times an uncertain concept. It is probably for this reason that the story is sometimes told of a young attorney who once made a legal argument before Oliver Wendell Holmes, Jr., one of the most famous judges in American history. When the attorney proclaimed that justice favored his client and that justice called for his client to be freed, Holmes responded "This is a court of law, young man, not a court of justice."[8] While this exchange may never have actually happened, it does reveal the tension between law and justice, and the importance of knowing the difference between the two.

The problem with law is that it can be unjust. In fact, one can say that law by its very nature is unjust. But if the injustice is too extreme, as it seemed to many people to be in the *Dudley* case, then society might lose trust in the legal system because it is achieving unjust results. In extreme cases this might even lead to revolution, as happened in America in 1776, or to civil war, which the country endured in the 1860s. So the legal system must always walk a fine line between law and justice.

The *Dudley* case showed the conflict between these two ideas in a way that still has lawyers and scholars debating today. The law of the case was clear, and according to that law, Dudley and Stephens were murderers who had to be hanged. But the facts of the case, the particular circumstances, were also gruesomely clear, and based on those facts, few people believed at the time, or believe today, that the two men deserved death. When the law and the facts (or to put it another way, law and justice) are so opposed to each other, the legal system faces a very difficult case. And as Holmes once wrote, "Hard cases make bad law."[9] But hard cases also make for excellent discussions about how the legal system works, and how it should work.

The *Dudley* case actually involves many more issues, ranging from the court's jurisdiction over the crime to the role of the jury, but these are technical legal questions. It is by these technical aspects of the law that the criminal system seeks to achieve justice.

2

The History of the Criminal Law

O. J. Simpson is one of the most famous sports figures in American history. A Heisman Trophy winner at the University of Southern California, Simpson was a star running back for the Buffalo Bills and San Francisco 49ers football teams throughout the 1970s. Even those with little interest in sports recognized Simpson from his starring roles in a number of major motion pictures as well as his appearance in a string of national rental car commercials.

But Simpson's fame has a sinister facet as well. During his marriage to Nicole Brown in the 1980s, police were called to the couple's home on more than one occasion because of Simpson's violent behavior, and in 1989 he was convicted of spousal abuse, having punched and slapped her, and sentenced to probation. Eventually the couple divorced, but other confrontations took place. Brown's friends stated that she believed that Simpson was stalking her, and some even said that Simpson had threatened to kill her if she ever became involved with another man.[1]

On the night of June 12, 1994, police found the bodies of Brown and her friend Ron Goldman outside Brown's Los Angeles home. Both Brown and Goldman had been savagely stabbed to death. Detectives soon began to focus their attention on Simpson. One nearby resident claimed to have spotted a car resembling Simpson's speeding away from the crime scene on the night of the killings; a cutlery store worker remembered selling Simpson a large knife a few weeks before the double homicide. Meanwhile, extensive DNA testing was underway on items from the crime scene and Simpson's home.

Within a week, police were prepared to arrest Simpson. They agreed to let Simpson turn himself in, but Simpson failed to appear at the police station. Tracing calls from Simpson's cell phone, officers began to move toward the fugitive's location.

One of the most bizarre events in the investigation began when police spotted Simpson riding in a car driven by his friend Al Cowlings and began a pursuit. Cowlings shouted at an officer that Simpson was holding a gun to his own head. Hearing this, the officer backed off, but he continued the chase, and soon a dozen more police cars had joined in. The chase continued for more than an hour. News helicopters provided aerial coverage of the drama, which television networks broadcast live to a national audience of nearly 100 million viewers. Thousands of people lined the streets where Cowlings and Simpson were expected to pass.

Eventually the car stopped at Simpson's home, and the fugitive went inside. He emerged in police custody an hour later, under arrest for the murders of Goldman and Brown.[2]

Simpson's trial lasted from January to October of 1995 and was the longest and most complex murder trial in California history. The **state** was represented by a number of prosecuting attorneys, while Simpson assembled a legal team that included some of the highest-profile lawyers in America, among them noted defense attorney F. Lee Bailey and Harvard law professor Alan Dershowitz. Dozens of expert witnesses testified, and the state's attorneys made heavy use of the relatively new science of DNA profiling to link Simpson to the murders.

The *Simpson* case was highly controversial for several reasons. Simpson's status as a celebrity drew heavy media attention both before and during the trial, an element that was further reinforced by the trial judge's decision to allow live national television coverage of the proceedings. The case's great complexity placed a heavy burden on prosecutors, but some of their most important potential witnesses were unable to testify because they had accepted payment for interviews they gave to reporters before the trial, which suggested that they may be biased. The most divisive element, however, was the issue of race. Simpson was

O. J. Simpson and one of his defense attorneys, F. Lee Bailey, left, consult with each other during the Simpson double-murder trial in Los Angeles. *AP Photo/Reed Saxon, Pool*

black, but his two victims, along with most of the main investigators and prosecutors, were white. (While most of Simpson's lawyers were also white, the African-American defense attorney Johnnie Cochran rose to national prominence during the trial.) The jury, moreover, included only two whites; nine of the remaining jurors were black and one was Latino. Perhaps none of these racial matters would have been of importance, however, until the defense lawyers managed to present evidence suggesting that Mark Fuhrman, a white police detective, had behaved in a racist manner.

According to Simpson's team, Fuhrman had planted a blood-stained glove at Simpson's home in order to incriminate him. When asked if he had recently used racial slurs to describe blacks, Fuhrman swore that he had not; but later the defense lawyers played an audio tape in which Fuhrman did just that. This evidence destroyed the officer's credibility and made the case seem like a racial attack on Simpson.

In addition to their racial arguments, Simpson's lawyers also tried to show that police had mishandled the DNA evidence from the crime scene. This was quite possible, and at any rate DNA profiling was still fairly new and primitive. For all of these reasons, the DNA evidence, which can be highly conclusive in modern cases, had little impact in the Simpson proceedings.

At the conclusion of the months-long trial, the jury took only four hours before finding Simpson not guilty. This verdict immediately caused a national outcry, with citizens dividing sharply along racial lines between those who were sure that Simpson had killed Goldman and Brown, and those who thought that the investigation had not been reliable.

A basic doctrine of American criminal law is that a person cannot be tried twice for the same crime, a concept known as **double jeopardy**. But Simpson did undergo a second trial a year later. This trial, however, did not bring about double jeopardy. Once the first jury had acquitted Simpson, in fact, he could never again be tried for the murders of Goldman and Brown, even if he were to admit later that he *had* killed them. And in 2006 he wrote a book entitled *If I Did It*, in which he seemed to many people to confess. In this book he described how he would have gone about killing the couple if he had in fact been the murderer. Because he had already been found not guilty of the crime, he was in no danger from the criminal law by saying such things.

What, then, was the basis for the second trial? It was the result of lawsuits by Brown's next of kin and Goldman's parents on the grounds of wrongful death—the argument that in killing Brown and Goldman, Simpson had cost their families money due to salaries that they would never be able to earn, and the value of the pain and suffering their deaths had caused them. And in this trial, the new jury found that Simpson *had* killed Brown and Goldman and ordered him to pay $33 million to Goldman's family and $12 million to Brown's.

In light of the ban on double jeopardy, how was Simpson able to be tried a second time? And, just as important, how could the two juries reach opposite conclusions? The answer lies in the very different nature of the two trials. The first was a **criminal trial**, a case brought by the state of California and its citizens against Simpson in an attempt to convict and punish him for the crime of murder. But the second was a **civil trial**, a proceeding not by the state but by private parties—the families of Goldman and Brown—in order to prove that he legally owed them money for causing their relatives' deaths. In this second trial, the jury could not send Simpson to jail; it could only require him to pay money to compensate the victims' families for their loss.

This difference also explains how the juries could reach opposite results. In American criminal trials, the prosecution must prove the defendant to be guilty **beyond a reasonable doubt**, which is a very high standard to meet. If a reasonable person could have reasonable doubt about the defendant's guilt, then the jury must find him or her to be not guilty. (One reason for this high standard is the concept, stated often throughout history, that "It is better that ten guilty persons escape than one innocent suffer."[3])

In a civil trial, the standard of proof is much lower, partly because the stakes are not those of freedom versus imprisonment, or even life versus death. While the **plaintiff** (the private party who is the civil trial counterpart of the prosecution) still has the burden of proving that the defendant is liable, he or she must do so only by a **preponderance of the evidence**. The preponderance standard only requires that the plaintiff show that it is *more likely than not* that the defendant is to blame—that is, more than a 50 percent likelihood. This is a much easier test to meet than the reasonable doubt standard, which is probably somewhere near the 100 percent mark.

O. J. Simpson's two trials, with their different outcomes, tell a great deal about the role of the criminal law in society, not just in America but throughout Western history. To understand how such results are possible, it is necessary to examine that history closely.

THE NATURE AND ROLE OF LAW IN SOCIETY

The word *law* can have many different meanings. Scientific laws describe regular and repeatable events in the physical world. Philosophers sometimes speak of the natural law as a set of universal principles that govern human nature. Some religions also set forth laws that they see as divinely inspired rules for proper living.

Even within the legal world, "law" means different things. It can refer to the legal system as a whole—that is, the government system for settling legal disputes between its citizens—or a particular rule within that system, such as the law that prohibits murder or the law setting speed limits. "Law" may also refer to the legal doctrine involving certain subjects, such as the law of contracts or the law of real property. "Law" may further describe even broader areas; for instance, the O. J. Simpson proceedings involved both a criminal trial, involving the subject of criminal law, and a civil trial, which was governed by the civil law. In addition to the civil and criminal law, there are also areas such as equity, a body of law that attempts to modify the rules of common law with principles of fairness, and admiralty, which involves maritime activities such as commerce and passenger ships, each field of law having its own rules and subjects. But in the broadest sense, all of these are still part of the overall system called "the law."

In most English-speaking countries, including Canada and the United States, one of the most important distinctions that lawyers and judges make is between the different sources of law—that is, the places they look to find legal rules. Law may be found in legislative enactments called **statutes**; in judges' written decisions of cases (**case law**); in **constitutions**, the highest government statements of written law; and in the rules that government agencies set forth, which are called **administrative regulations**. Because in the United States the federal government, as well as each state, has all four of these things, there are a great many sources of law in the United States. This number is made even higher by the fact that most cities, towns, and counties in America have their own local laws and regulations. To understand the criminal law, one must understand the differences among these basic sources as well as how they relate to each other.

Most English-speaking countries have a legal system based on the **common law**, which they inherited from England. To understand how the common law system works, it is necessary to learn something about English legal history. This, in turn, requires looking briefly at some legal systems that are older than England's.

EARLY LAW CODES

Even the most primitive societies have legal systems—that is, rules for settling disputes and letting members of the society know what they can and cannot do. These rules do not have to be written down. Because the facts of every case are different, it may be hard or impossible to write down a rule ahead of time that will cover every set of facts, or to know which rule will apply to a given dispute. For these reasons, unwritten law, or **custom**, plays an important role in many legal and criminal systems. Nevertheless, many early societies did write down their most important legal rules, sometimes in a highly organized fashion. These organized rule statements are known as **codes**. To this day a set of legal rules on a specific subject (such as the subject of criminal law) is referred to as a code.

The earliest codes were written thousands of years ago in the Middle East, where the earliest civilizations emerged. One of these, the Codex of Lipit-Ishtar, dates to nearly 2000 years B.C. The more famous Code of Hammurabi, named after the Babylonian king who set it forth, is nearly as old. Despite being 3,700 years old, some of its laws sound very much like modern criminal statutes. One paragraph, for instance, gives a definition of burglary surprisingly similar to the modern notion, although the punishment is much greater: "If a man make a breach in a house," it reads, "they shall put him to death in front of that breach and they shall thrust him therein." Another provision, very similar to modern laws against robbery or piracy, declares that "If a man practice brigandage and be captured, that man shall be put to death."[4]

Oddly, the very fact that Hammurabi allowed the code to be written down limited his powers as king. By being written down, the law existed independently of Hammurabi himself, in a way that meant his subjects could look to the code and know the law before they acted, without looking to the king. If the king kept his word, as written in the code, then he was bound to obey the law like everyone else. If he did not plan to keep his word, then there was no point in his writing the code to begin with. This was an important step toward a development known as **due process of law**. Due process is the concept that in criminal and noncriminal law, the government itself, just like individual citizens, must follow clear legal rules.

Another important development appeared in the most famous code of the ancient world: the Ten Commandments of the Hebrew Bible (the Old Testament). More than a legal code, the Decalogue, as the commandments are known, is a set of rules that the Hebrews declared were

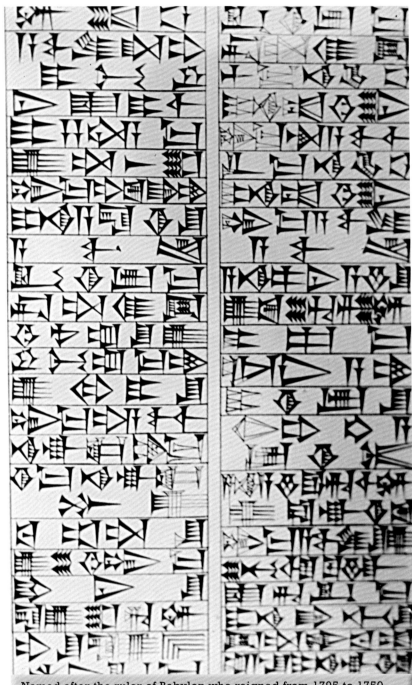

Named after the ruler of Babylon who reigned from 1795 to 1750 B.C., the Code of Hammurabi is one of the earliest systems of law. *Kean Collection/Getty Images*

set forth by God to govern their relations with him and with each other. Unlike most other ancient codes, the source of the commandments was believed to be God himself rather than human beings. Because of this fact, the Decalogue can be seen as an early type of **natural law**—a universal law, usually unwritten, that applies to all of humanity and is superior to all human-made law. Later generations would often argue that if human law violated the natural law (whether expressed in the Decalogue or in some other way), then the human laws were invalid. A famous echo of this in American history is to be found in the Declaration of Independence, in which Thomas Jefferson wrote that humans "are endowed by their Creator with certain unalienable rights" including the rights to "life, liberty, and the pursuit of happiness."

Still another famous law code of the Classical world was the Law of the Twelve Tables, compiled in the early years of the Roman Republic, around 480 B.C. According to tradition, Roman scholars traveled far and worked long to produce this code, which contained the very best rules from Roman and other societies. The Twelve Tables became a foundation of Roman law. Because Roman civilization lasted for nearly a thousand years and reached from the British Isles to Africa and the Middle East, Roman law had a widespread impact on Western, and even non-Western, legal thought. In fact, modern legal systems that are based on law codes are known interchangeably as code law, civil law, or Roman law systems. Today most of the non-English-speaking world relies to at least some extent on this type of system.

CUSTOM AND THE COMMON LAW

From the beginning of civilization there was another type of legal system as well. This second system was based heavily not on law codes but on the unwritten custom of the community, set forth by community leaders on a case-by-case basis. This was the usual approach among the Germanic tribes of Northern Europe, whom the Romans called barbarians. In the Roman view, this reliance on custom was more primitive and more arbitrary than was the case with legal codes. The final legal decisions between disputing parties rested with Germanic tribal leaders or chieftains who might be more concerned with their own welfare than with fair or legal results. Nevertheless, customary law, like code law, was to play a huge role in western legal development. This was especially true in the parts of Europe where Roman government was the weakest and lasted the shortest time, particularly in present-day England.

As more barbarian tribes moved from Asia into Europe and the Roman Empire began to disintegrate in the early Christian era, a new civilization began to emerge. Consisting of Roman, German, and Christian elements, the medieval world blended the ingredients of these three cultures in new and interesting ways. One of these ways was in a new set of law codes called the **Leges Barbarorum**, or the Laws of the Barbarians. These codes were the result of the Germanic tribes attempting to write their customary laws into Roman-style codes. At the same time the Catholic Church, which was nearly the only institution of the ancient world to survive the fall of the Roman Empire, gradually established courts of its own, called ecclesiastical courts. Over the next several hundred years, these church courts established their own set of laws, which became known as **canon law**. Meanwhile, local communities and important noblemen were developing their own court systems and laws. To the east, the Byzantine emperor Justinian, in the sixth century set forth the last great law code of the classical world—the Justinian code or the **Corpus Juris Civilis**—but this code remained almost unknown in western and northern Europe for the next thousand years.

In the regions that would later become Italy, Germany, France, and England, the law during the Middle Ages—the period from roughly 500 to 1500—was a patchwork of half-remembered Roman law, German tribal custom, and ecclesiastical law. Because the printing press did not appear until the 1400s, and most people were unable to read or write, much of the law remained unwritten, and the law varied widely from place to place.

One widespread concept was the **wergild**—literally, the "man price"—that set forth the compensation that one person must pay another in exchange for various types of injury to another. The price would vary depending on the type of injury as well as the social status, and thus the basic value, of the person who was injured. An injury to a warrior, for instance, would be worth a high price, while an injury to an elderly woman might be worth little or nothing. In a sense, the wergild is a type of early criminal law, since it dealt with penalties for injuries, but both the injuries and the prices to be paid for them were of a private nature, owed from one member of society directly to another (although by command of the lawgiver). The law existed merely to set forth and to enforce the payment.[5]

While code law remained important on continental Europe, customary law remained dominant in England, where Roman rule had never been strong. But in England, as elsewhere, the patchwork of local and feudal courts was so complex that there was no unified law or court system for hundreds of years.

This began changing in the eleventh century. In 1066, Duke William of Normandy invaded England in order to claim his rights to the English throne. Soon Duke William had become King William the Conqueror. Before his death in 1087, William had set up an efficient central government that enabled him to extend his control throughout the country.

In the 1100s one of William's great-grandchildren, King Henry II, extended this central control to the legal system. Henry was distressed by the wasteful private feuds that were taking place among his subjects, destroying valuable property and claiming lives. He also resented his lack of control over the various courts. So Henry set up a new national court system, known as the royal courts. The judges he appointed to these courts traveled throughout England, hearing and deciding cases quickly and efficiently. Because the royal judges wrote down their rulings in these cases, they used these written judicial opinions to guide their decisions in later, similar cases, in the same way as other judges might turn to codes. In this way, then, the royal judges began to write community customs into English law. Because the judges applied these same opinions and customs throughout England, they became something the entire country's law shared in common. Thus, the written judicial opinions of the royal judges became known as the common law.

Today the major legal systems of the world fall into one of two categories. Most countries use a code law system, which relies heavily on codes or statutes, usually written today not by an individual lawgiver but by a legislative assembly. In code law systems, a judge's decision in a criminal or a civil law case usually has importance only for the parties involved in that case.

Instead of code law, England and countries with an English heritage, such as the United States, Canada, Australia, New Zealand, and others, use the common law system. In this system, unlike in the code law system, the written opinions of judges are as important as statutes, because these opinions serve as binding **precedent** in later, similar cases, which means that judges in later cases must abide by the rulings of the judges in earlier cases.

THE BEGINNING OF THE MODERN CRIMINAL LAW

The common law soon involved many different types of relationships in medieval England. Trade, personal injuries, the transfer of property, and marriage were some of the major areas. Soon, however, the common law began to distinguish between actions for private injuries and punishment for injuries to the public as a whole. This separation of private from public wrongdoing was the beginning of modern criminal law.

The emphasis of the old wergild system was on private payments to persons who had suffered because of another's wrongful conduct. If Hengist injured or killed Horsa either accidentally or intentionally, then according to wergild, Horsa or his family could demand payment from Hengist to compensate for the loss, much as the Brown and Goldman families sought money from O. J. Simpson. But as England's new rulers established their power after William's conquest, they expanded the notion of the king's peace. According to this idea, if Hengist's injury to Horsa somehow disturbed this peace, then Hengist had to answer not just to Horsa, but to the king. This is one of the basic notions underlying the modern criminal law system; that the criminal law exists to protect society, not merely the individual victim, from a criminal's wrongdoing. Today, one obvious example of this is how court cases are named. Even the names of the cases involving O. J. Simpson are an example: While the lawsuit by Nicole Brown Simpson's next of kin was entitled *Brown v. Simpson*,[6] the criminal case against the football player bore the name *People v. Simpson.*[7]

It was not only specific conduct that became criminal. During this same time, various ways of identifying, accusing, and trying criminal wrongdoers also developed. One of the most important of these is the **grand jury**. Because the citizens of a local community were most likely to know the facts of a case as well as the reputations and characters of the parties, royal judges began to hear reports of crimes and suspected crimes from local groups known as inquests. Inquests—later called grand inquests—eventually developed into the modern grand jury, which investigates suspected crimes. Today, in American federal courts as well as many state courts, an **indictment** or formal accusation by a grand jury is needed in order to try persons for major crimes.

In medieval England, after being charged with a crime by a grand inquest, the accused eventually began to claim the right to have a second inquest investigate the charges in order to decide whether he or she was actually guilty. This second inquest later developed into the

FELONY AND MISDEMEANOR

In the common law system, crimes are either **felonies** or **misdemeanors**. Traditionally, a felony is any crime that is punishable by death or by a term of more than one year in prison, and all other crimes are misdemeanors. The difference is important for several reasons. For instance, a crime may make reference to another crime in its definition. Burglary is defined as breaking and entering into a building at night with an intent to commit a felony—not a misdemeanor—inside. The law may allow or require harsher sentences for criminals who have previously been convicted of more than one felony, but not for criminals who have committed only misdemeanors. Finally, some states may bar convicted felons, after completing their prison sentences, from voting, holding public office, or serving as attorneys. For these reasons, felonies are obviously more serious crimes than misdemeanors, and it is necessary to know the difference between the two types of crime.

petit jury or **trial jury**, which today is the jury that gives the verdict of "guilty" or "not guilty." The various rules for trying a criminal case before this jury also evolved until they, too, developed into our modern system. All of these rules for investigating crimes and trying suspected criminals form a subject known as **criminal procedure**. Many rules of criminal procedure, such as those requiring the use of grand juries and petit juries, appear in the United States Constitution's **Bill of Rights**.

THE ROLE OF STATUTES IN THE COMMON LAW SYSTEM

While the common law courts and the judicial opinions and precedents they set forth are still a highly important source of law in any common law system, statutes, or acts of legislative assemblies, also play an important role. As the medieval period gave way to the modern era in England, the king's council of advisors gradually evolved into the modern legislature known as Parliament. (The name probably comes from the word parley, which means to bargain or haggle, which describes how a legislature often works.) Parliament, as well as later legislatures such as Congress or state general assemblies, enacts statutes, or legislation, that are just as much a part of the law as judicial opinions are. Therefore, in a common law country, to know the law on any given subject—such as the law of murder or burglary—one must know not only what the courts have declared, but what legislatures have said in their statutes.

This can sometimes be difficult. For instance, a legislature can modify a common law rule, in effect declaring that "Rule R, as set forth by court C, may have been the law until now, but we hereby change rule R into Rule S, which shall apply from now on." On the other hand, courts are usually free not only to set forth and explain community custom, but also to explain the meaning of, or **interpret**, a legislature's statutes—including how those statutes affect the common law. In the above example, then, the court may have the last word as to what Rule S actually means. This makes the relationship between judicial opinions and statutes a dynamic one that is constantly changing.

This was the state of the law in England at the time of the founding of England's colonies in North America. At first, colonial governments and societies were primitive, with very basic courts and legislatures, few libraries and printing presses, and practically no lawyers. But as colonial societies grew, they naturally tended to copy the rules and institutions of the mother country. This meant that the colonial legal systems followed the common law. They were aided in this by the publication, in the 1760s, of a four-volume work by the English scholar Sir William Blackstone, *Commentaries on the Laws of England*. Blackstone's *Commentaries* summarized both the common law and the most important laws of Parliament in a short, easy-to-use format and greatly strengthened the impact of the common law in the colonies even as the American Revolution burst over the country. One entire volume of the *Commentaries*, moreover, deals entirely with the criminal law.

Largely because of Blackstone's influence, many state governments passed "reception statutes" after the revolution that formally adopted the common law as it existed in 1776. As a result, the common law is the main legal system within the United States, except for a handful of states (most especially Louisiana, which was a long-time colony of France and Spain with their code law traditions).

In the late 1800s, with the coming of the Industrial Revolution and the new social problems it created, statute law began to grow in importance throughout the United States. Because of the need to adapt quickly to problems of new, city-based industrial life—problems such as increased crime, dangerous working conditions, and greater threats of fire and disease—Congress as well as the state legislatures began to enact more statutes than before, and on a wider variety of subjects. This trend has continued to the present day, making statutes a more important source of law than ever before in common law systems.

As part of this development, the executive branch of government—headed by the president at the national level and governors at the state level—also expanded to deal with modern problems. Today, the federal and state executive branches have a great many agencies dedicated to the areas of public health, criminal justice, environmental and workplace regulation, and many more fields. These agencies have the power to enact administrative regulations that, like judicial decisions and statutes, have the force of law. Like statutes, these regulations may impose criminal penalties on individuals who fail to abide by them. Also like statutes, they are subject to interpretation by courts.

The huge number of statutes in recent decades, and the various approaches to crime that different states have taken, prompted a group of legal scholars to set forth a modern code of criminal law as a guideline for legislatures. In 1962 they completed work on the **Model Penal Code**, a systematic approach to criminal law to be used as a guide by lawmakers nationwide. Although the Model Penal Code is not law, many of its rules have been grafted into criminal statutes in different states. In this way, then, the attempt to codify the law begun thousands of years ago by Lipit-Ishtar and Hammurabi continues.

The Criminal Law and the American Federal System

Clarence Earl Gideon was a drifter. Born in Missouri in 1910, he had often run afoul of the law. He had even served time in the federal penitentiary in Leavenworth, Kansas. Now in Panama City, Florida, in 1961, he was in trouble again.

Early on the morning of June 3, Henry Cook, who knew Gideon, was coming home from a dance in a nearby town when he walked past a poolroom just a few doors down from Gideon's home. Looking in the poolroom's window, Cook later claimed, he saw Gideon inside, apparently drunk, with his pockets bulging. When police were summoned, they found no sign of Gideon, but they did discover signs that someone had entered the building through the back window and had stolen money and liquor. Based on this evidence and Cook's story, the police arrested Gideon for the burglary.

Because Gideon had once been tried and convicted in a federal court, he knew that the Sixth Amendment to the United States Constitution gave him the right to be represented by an attorney (or, in the words of the amendment, "**assistance of counsel**"). But the Bill of Rights—the first ten amendments to the Constitution—only gave citizens rights against the federal, or national, government, and not against the state governments. The burglary with which Gideon was

43

charged was a crime under the laws of Florida, not a federal crime, so although he could not afford a lawyer, the state refused to appoint one to represent him. When the day of his trial arrived, this caused some trouble.

The first few moments of the court proceedings were routine.

"Are you ready to go to trial in this case?" Judge Robert L. McCrary, Jr. asked the prosecutor.

"The state is ready, your honor," the government lawyer answered.

"What says the Defendant?" asked McCrary. "Are you ready to go to trial?"

That was when things started going wrong. "I am not ready, your honor," said Gideon.

"Why aren't you ready?"

"I have no counsel," explained Gideon.

"Why do you not have counsel?" McCrary inquired. "Did you not know your trial was set for today?"

"Yes, sir," replied Gideon. "I know it was set for today."

"Why, then, did you not secure counsel and be prepared to go to trial?" repeated the judge.

"Your honor," said Gideon, "I request this Court to appoint counsel to represent me in this trial."

"Mr. Gideon, I am sorry," stated McCrary, "but I cannot appoint counsel to represent you in this case. Under the laws of the state of Florida, the only time the court can appoint counsel to represent a Defendant is when that person is charged with a capital offense." (A capital offense is one punishable by death, and that was not the case here.)[1]

Because of McCrary's ruling, Gideon had to defend himself in his trial. His opponent was a lawyer with a professional education and years of courtroom experience. It is not surprising, then, that Gideon found himself outmatched. The jury convicted him of breaking and entering, and the court sentenced him to a five-year prison term.[2]

From jail, Gideon handwrote a petition to the Supreme Court of the United States, perhaps getting some help from a fellow convict who had once been a lawyer himself. In this petition, Gideon told the Supreme Court that he had been denied the assistance of counsel, and he asked the justices to review his case. Two months later, the court agreed.

DIVISION OF CORRECTIONS

CORRESPONDENCE REGULATIONS

MAIL WILL NOT BE DELIVERED WHICH DOES NOT CONFORM WITH THESE RULES

No. 1 -- Only 2 letters each week, not to exceed 2 sheets letter-size 8 1/2 x 11" and written *on one side only*, and if ruled paper, do not write between lines. *Your complete name* must be signed at the close of your letter. *Clippings, stamps, letters* from other people, *stationery or cash must not be enclosed* in your letters.

No. 2 -- All *letters* must be addressed in the *complete prison name* of the inmate. Cell *number*, where applicable, and *prison number* must be placed in lower left corner of envelope, with your complete name and address in the upper left corner.

No. 3 -- *Do not send any packages without a Package Permit.* Unauthorized *packages* will be destroyed.

No. 4 -- *Letters* must be written in English only.

No. 5 -- *Books, magazines, pamphlets,* and *newspapers* of reputable character will be delivered *only if* mailed direct from the publisher.

No. 6 -- *Money* must be sent in the form of *Postal Money Orders* only, in the inmate's complete prison name and prison number.

INSTITUTION _____   CELL NUMBER _____

NAME _____   NUMBER _____

In The Supreme Court of The United States
Washington D.C.

Clarence Earl Gideon
    Petitioner

vs.

H.G. Cochran, Jr, as
Director, Divisions
of corrections State
of Florida

Petition for a writ
of Certiorari Directed
to The Supreme Court
State of Florida.

No. **890** Misc.

OCT. TERM 1961
U. S. Supreme Court

To. The Honorable Earl Warren, Chief
Justice of the United States

    Comes now The petitioner, Clarence
Earl Gideon, a citizen of The United states
of America, in proper person, and appearing
as his own counsel. Who petitions this
Honorable Court for a Writ of Certiorari
directed to The Supreme Court of The State
of Florida. To review the order and Judge-
ment of the court below denying The
petitioner a writ of Habeus Corpus.

    Petitioner submits That The Supreme
Court of The United States has The authority
and jurisdiction to review The final Judge-
ment of The Supreme Court of The State
of Florida The highest court of The State
Under sec. 344(B) Title 28 U.S.C.A. and
Because the "Due process clause" of the

The Supreme Court's response to this handwritten petition by Clarence Earl Gideon gave all criminal defendants the right to an attorney. *MPI/Getty Images*

What happened next was one of a series of steps in a constitutional revolution. The Supreme Court appointed Abe Fortas, an expert attorney with an excellent reputation (and who would later become a Supreme Court justice himself), to represent Gideon, and it heard arguments on behalf of both Gideon and Florida. In 1963, in the case of *Gideon v. Wainwright*, it ruled that the Sixth Amendment's right to assistance of counsel in all criminal cases applied in state criminal trials as well as in federal ones.

Because of this ruling, Gideon's conviction was thrown out. A new trial was held in Florida state court, this time with Gideon having a lawyer's assistance. The lawyer showed Henry Cook to be an unreliable witness whose word could not be trusted. Based on this showing, the jury found Gideon not guilty.[3]

The case's importance, however, went far beyond that. Until this moment, the only time a criminal defendant had a federally guaranteed right to counsel was when he or she was accused of a federal crime, or when the state crime he or she was accused of carried the death penalty. But the great majority of criminal trials are for violations of state offenses, most of them noncapital. Until Gideon's case, then, most criminal defendants had no constitutional right to an attorney. But because of *Gideon v. Wainwright*, all criminal defendants since then—federal and state, in both capital and noncapital cases—have the right to an attorney even when they cannot afford to pay for one. Throughout the country, attorneys known as **public defenders** stand ready to represent criminal defendants.

The *Gideon* case reveals the very important distinction between federal and state laws. This division of authority between the national and state governments is a concept known as **federalism**, and it is a major element of the American constitutional and legal systems. This chapter will explore how, and why, federalism came to be, along with other important aspects of the Constitution, including separation of powers and the role of the Bill of Rights.

EARLY FOUNDATIONS OF AMERICAN GOVERNMENT

England's 13 North American colonies were founded over a long period, between 1607 and 1733, and each colony developed under its own particular circumstances. Virginia, for example, began as a business venture in the early 17th century. While Massachusetts, first settled between 1620 and 1630, was originally intended as a refuge for religious dissenters, Georgia, founded a hundred years after Massachusetts, was set up largely as a military defense zone to protect colonies to its north from Spanish settlements to its south. As a result, each colony had its own culture, its own social system, and its own laws.

Because there was no overall national government within North America during the colonial period, the individual colonial governments were very important. And because each colony had a relatively small population whose members tended to share the same cultural outlook, ways of making a living, and even extended family relations, each colonial government was relatively accessible and responsive to the needs of its citizens. Disputes over government did sometimes arise within a colony, but only rarely did they become major problems.

Yet the colonial governments did have many things in common with each other. One was their national government—a government based not in Washington, D.C. (for there was no such city in colonial times), but in London, England. For the most part, the central government in England let each colony govern itself, although it did exercise a small amount of overall control. Another thing the colonies shared was their legal heritage. Being English in origin, each colony naturally followed the mother country's example when forming its own legal and government systems. Just as England had the common law, therefore, so too did the colonies. As England had a king (or sometimes a queen), each colony had a governor, often one appointed by the crown. As England had Parliament, so too did each colony have a legislature.

By 1400, Parliament was divided into two houses (an arrangement known as **bicameralism**, which literally means "two chambers"). One, the House of Lords, consisted of titled nobility such as dukes, earls, and barons. The other, the House of Commons, was made up of commoners, that is, English subjects who held no titles of nobility. Likewise, most of the colonies developed an assembly, or lower house, elected by the voters at large, and a council, consisting of some of the colony's leading citizens. This council functioned as an upper house as well as an advisory group to the governor. The council might even serve as the colony's highest court. That court, together with the other colonial courts, followed the common law as well as other English legal traditions.

The American Revolution of the 1760s and the 1770s took place because Parliament, for a variety of reasons, began to exercise more active control over affairs in the colonies. After having had their way for so long, many colonists resented the new policy and claimed that Parliament was violating historical principles of the unwritten English Constitution. Colonists especially disliked being under the control of a distant central government that contained no representatives from the colonies. (This is the basis for the famous saying, "No taxation without representation.") Colonists also objected to new criminal procedures adopted by British officials. Among these were writs of assistance, or general search warrants that allowed officials to enter any private building during daylight hours in order to search for smuggled goods. Later, as tensions between the colonies and London increased, Parliament even allowed the king's officials to transfer colonists who were charged with crimes to England for trial. This would involve dangerous and expensive voyages to and from England, where the defendant would have great trouble furnishing witnesses and evidence in his or her defense. Eventually, uniting in common cause, the colonies declared themselves independent from England in 1776.

In the years following 1776, Americans drew heavily on their recent experiences with England as they organized their new state and national governments. One of the most important developments was that each state approved a written constitution—a document that formed the most basic law within the state, with which all other state laws had to agree. Because the debates over the unwritten English Constitution had ultimately led to war between England and the colonies, Americans wanted no such misunderstandings among themselves in the future. Instead, they tried to write down in their state constitutions exactly what powers the state governments did and did not have.

The new state constitutions established governments that, for the most part, resembled the colonial governments and even the English government itself. In order to grant the state government enough power to govern effectively while preventing it from abusing its power, states followed the principle of **separation of powers**. This simply means that no one person, or group of people, can control all of a government's powers. Most state constitutions established three separate branches of government: a bicameral legislature to enact laws; an executive branch headed by a governor to put those laws into effect; and a judicial branch, consisting of various courts, to hear and decide cases between citizens, or between a citizen and the government. In the case of any uncertainty about the exact meaning of a statute, a common law doctrine, or even a passage in the state constitution, the courts also had the power to decide on and explain the correct meaning so that it would be clear in the future.

Having set up these safeguards of written constitutions and separation of powers, citizens continued to have a fair amount of trust in their state governments for the same reasons they always had trusted their colonial governments The state governments had also helped lead the fight against England. It was the idea of a powerful central, or national, government—one located beyond a state's boundaries and with little representation by that state—that most worried American citizens.

Nevertheless, soon after the revolution's end, Americans realized that they did need a central government that had some basic powers, such as the need to oversee national and international trade and to maintain armed forces to protect the country. In order to do these things, moreover, the national government would need to be able to pay for them, which meant that it would need to tax citizens (a very touchy subject in the wake of the revolution). So in 1787, delegates from most of the states met in Philadelphia to set up a national government with these powers.

In creating a new national system that they did not fully trust, the founders naturally relied on the safeguards that they had also set up at the state level. The basis of government was to be a written constitution—the same Constitution of the United States that is in effect today—and it, too, would establish a framework based on separation of powers, in this case one that consisted of a president, a bicameral Congress composed of a Senate and a House of Representatives, and a national judicial system headed by the United States Supreme Court.

The founders added another important safeguard as well: the principle of federalism. This was based on the simple fact that the state

governments and constitutions continued to exist; the state governments would retain their full authority except in subjects where the
national Constitution transferred power to the national government. In
fact, for decades to come, the state governments would be more active
and important than the new national government, and in some ways,
such as in the field of criminal law, they continue to be.

While simple in theory, federalism is a detailed and sometimes difficult process. The founders wrote a short but important list of powers
the national government was to have, including the power to regulate
national and foreign trade, the power to coin money, the power to
maintain armed forces and to declare war, and, of course, the power to
levy taxes.[4] (Especially important for our purposes was the power to
enact national criminal laws.) The understanding was that if a power
did not appear in this list or elsewhere in the Constitution, the national
government could not exercise that power. This was an important limi-
tation designed to keep the national government from exercising too
much authority.

States, on the other hand, tended to have a much wider range of
power, some of which they shared with the national government, such
as the power to tax and the power to establish criminal laws. But what if
a national law somehow came into conflict with a state power? A clause
in the national Constitution provided that "This Constitution, and the
Laws of the United States which shall be made in Pursuance thereof; and
all Treaties made, or which shall be made, under the Authority of the
United States, shall be the supreme Law of the Land." This **Supremacy
Clause**, as it is known, meant that if such conflicts arose, the national,
or federal, law would stand and the state law would give way. Nevertheless, the great bulk of government power remained with the states. Even
today, for example, more than 90 percent of criminal prosecutions take
place in state, not federal, courts.[5]

In addition to drawing up a list of things that the federal government
could do, the authors of the Constitution also wrote a brief list of things
that the central government could *not* do. To this they added another
short list of things that the *state* governments could not do. The most
important of these restrictions deal with the criminal law. According
to these provisions, neither the state nor the national government may

pass an *ex post facto* **law**, which is a law that criminally punishes actions that citizens took before the law's passage. (For instance, if today a state reduced the speed limit from 60 to 35 miles per hour, citizens cannot be prosecuted for having driven 60 miles per hour last week.) The Constitution also bars both the state and national governments from passing a **bill of attainder**—a law that criminally punishes a citizen or declares him or her guilty without permitting him or her a trial. Finally, the Constitution prevents the national government from suspending a writ, or court order, known as **habeas corpus**, except in certain narrow circumstances. This is a court order to someone (usually a law officer) requiring him or her to show the court what legal authority he or she has for holding someone in custody. If prisoners (including those who have been accused of a crime

JURISDICTION

Jurisdiction is a broad term in law. Literally meaning "to speak the law" or "to say what the law is," jurisdiction refers to the authority of a particular court to hear and decide a case. A court's jurisdiction may be limited in several ways. Juvenile courts, for example, only have jurisdiction in cases involving children under the age of 18. An appellate court may only have jurisdiction to hear an appeal from a trial court, and not the jurisdiction to try a case itself. The courts of one state may only have jurisdiction over criminal offenses committed within the territory of that state. Jurisdiction can also be used more loosely, such as when a law enforcement officer of one state observes that he or she does not have the jurisdiction to make an arrest in another state, or even when someone refers to two different states or counties as different jurisdictions.

An interesting part of the American federal system is that the federal and state governments both have jurisdiction over the same people in the same geographic area. The people of Wisconsin, for instance, are under the jurisdiction of both the Wisconsin government and the United States government, including federal and state laws, law officers, and courts. The same is true in every other state.

but not yet tried) did not have access to this **writ**, then law officers could hold them without trial, for any or no reason, for as long as the officers wished. The writ of habeas corpus, then, gives courts supervision over the criminal justice system in order to prevent abuses within that system.[6]

THE BILL OF RIGHTS

Even the limitations of separation of powers and federalism, however, were not enough for most Americans. In 1787 and 1788, as the state governments debated whether to accept the new national Constitution, many people wanted a longer, more complete list of things that the federal government could not do as an additional protection of individual rights. Some states refused to accept the new Constitution unless such a list were to be added. As a result, one of Congress's very first actions under the new government was to prepare a list of amendments, known as the Bill of Rights, to add to the original Constitution. The states accepted the new amendments by 1791.

Along with the notion of a written constitution, separation of powers, and federalism, the Bill of Rights is one of the most important devices for controlling power in the system of American government. These ten amendments, particularly the First Amendment, list many of Americans' most basic freedoms, such as freedom of expression, a prohibition on an established religion, and the right to free exercise of religion. In the area of criminal law, the Fourth, Fifth, Sixth, and Eighth Amendments contain important safeguards to protect prisoners, criminal defendants, and those who are under police investigation. These safeguards include a prohibition on unreasonable searches or seizures; the right of accused persons to a speedy and public trial by jury; and the right to the assistance of counsel. The Fifth Amendment also contains the famous Due Process Clause, which embodies the ancient idea that the government must obey the law. According to this clause, "No person shall ... be deprived of life, liberty, or property, without due process of law."

An interesting, and important, fact about the Bill of Rights is that originally it gave citizens protections only against the national government, not the state governments. This meant, for instance, that in a trial in federal court for a violation of a federal criminal law, a

The Bill of Rights was created to provide additional protection of individual rights against encroachment by the federal government. *AP Photo/National Archives*

defendant had a right to an attorney, as set forth by the Sixth Amendment. But the Sixth Amendment did not give defendants the right to an attorney in a trial before a state court for a violation of state criminal law. The reason for this difference should be obvious: It was the national government that Americans most feared, because of their experiences with Parliament; they were less distrustful of their state governments, which they could more easily control. (State constitutions, in fact, usually contain their own bills of rights, although sometimes the exact rights listed differ from those set forth in the federal version.)

As time passed, however, citizens' views of the state governments changed. One of the most important reasons for this change was the issue of slavery.

Like many other subjects, such as marriage and divorce, inheritance, and property conveyance, slavery was a matter of state, not national, law. The federal Constitution recognized that a state might choose to allow slavery and to give slave owners certain rights, but whether or not a state did choose to do so was up to that state's government and its voting citizens (who were almost all white, even in nonslave states.)

Before the American Revolution, most of the colonies allowed slavery. Afterward, as cotton became a huge cash crop, slavery died out in the colder northern states but expanded rapidly in the southern states, where it was crucial to large-scale cotton production.

In time, more and more American whites began to look down on slavery as being inconsistent with the principles of democracy. One northern group in particular, known as the Abolitionists, were very vocal in their calls for a national constitutional amendment to end slavery. Many southern whites, on the other hand, with their dependence on the cotton economy, found this idea unacceptable.

In the end, the conflict between pro- and anti-slave elements led to the Civil War of 1861–1865. As a direct result of the war, slavery came to an end with the ratification of the Thirteenth Amendment to the federal Constitution.

Because slavery had been allowed and defended by the state governments, many citizens (including the newly freed slaves) had come to see the states, and not the national government, as the main threat to liberty—an exact reversal of the traditional view. As a result of this changed opinion, the country also ratified the Fourteenth Amendment, which sharply limited some powers of the state governments. This is the single most important amendment to the federal Constitution, changing to a degree the relationship between the national and state governments.

One of the Fourteenth Amendment's most important clauses declares that all persons born within the United States are citizens. Another is a second Due Process Clause. The Fifth Amendment's due process provision applies only to the national government, but the Fourteenth Amendment's requires *state* governments to observe due process of law toward all persons.

The main purpose behind these new clauses was clear. Most northerners wanted to protect the newly freed slaves from the southern state governments, which were still mainly in white hands. But, in an ironic twist, the northern supporters of the amendment failed to realize that they themselves could discriminate. Soon, former slaves and their children began moving north, even as new waves of immigrants, mostly from central and eastern Europe, began to change the ethnic makeup of

America. The new immigrants, most of whom arrived in northern sea-
ports, had sharply different language, cultural, and religious practices
from the predominately Anglo-Saxon Protestant culture of the United
States. At times, these new immigrants, along with their children and
grandchildren, would face discrimination from established society in
both north and south. As time passed and these patterns became clear,
the federal courts, after years of inaction, gradually began to recognize
and to try to correct these problems.[7]

The Fourteenth Amendment Due Process Clause protects the "liberty" of individuals from violation by a state. Where is this "liberty"
spelled out and explained? How do people know exactly what the word
includes? The answer would seem to be the *federal* Bill of Rights, the
rights that Americans have against the national government. Because of
this reasoning, in the early twentieth century the federal courts began
to find that in light of the Fourteenth Amendment and its Due Process
Clause, the federal Bill of Rights now protected persons from state
governments as well as from the national government. In other words,
these courts found that the word *liberty* in the Fourteenth Amendment
incorporated, or included, most of the rights listed in the first ten
amendments.

This development did not happen all at once. The United States
Supreme Court took several decades to extend one right after another
to apply against the state governments. Most of the criminal provisions,
in particular, were not included until the 1950s and 1960s under Chief
Justice Earl Warren, the son of immigrants and who had once served
as a state prosecuting attorney. *Gideon v. Wainwright*, in which the
Supreme Court required the state governments to provide attorneys to
state criminal defendants, was just one of a long string of cases in this
process. Other famous cases include *Malloy v. Hogan*, which held that
state courts could not force persons to incriminate themselves; *Benton
v. Maryland*, which bars state courts from subjecting persons to double
jeopardy; and *Duncan v. Louisiana*, which gives defendants in state
criminal trials a federal right to a trial by jury.[8]

A few clauses in the federal Bill of Rights that are related to criminal matters continue to apply only to the federal and not the state
governments. One of these is the Fifth Amendment clause requiring

indictments, or formal criminal charges against defendants, to be handed down by a grand jury. Although most states do make use of grand juries, the federal Constitution does not require them to do so. Another is the federal prohibition on excessive bail that is found in the Eighth Amendment.[9]

Today, as a result of the incorporation process, most of the Bill of Rights applies to both national and state action. While most Americans accept this as the standard without much thought, it is still a fairly recent development in the American constitutional and legal systems, especially in the area of criminal law. In state criminal trials, the protections of the Bill of Rights have applied for barely half a century. The incorporation of Bill of Rights provisions into the Fourteenth Amendment's Due Process Clause, then, has been one of the most important developments in the American criminal system.

The Process of Legislation

Legislation has played an increasingly important role in the American legal system during the last century and a half. This is partly because legislation can respond more quickly to new, changed conditions than common law, which tends to move more slowly in order to maintain stability. One example of legislative response to new social problems is the federal kidnapping statute.

The word *kidnapping* literally means nabbing, or snatching away, a child, although anyone may be kidnapped. It involves the carrying away of a victim by force or fraud against his will. The crime has been around for a very long time, but as the Industrial Revolution reached America in the mid-1800s, it suddenly became a highly visible menace.

By the 1870s, America's major cities were growing quickly as workers streamed in from the country and foreign nations to become factory employees. At the same time, high-speed transportation was developing as the railroad network expanded. By the 20th century, the automobile would become a major, and fast, means of travel. This large and ever-moving population meant that criminals could work with anonymity and make fast getaways. And because some industrial figures and investors were becoming very wealthy during the Industrial Revolution, the idea of ransoms began to appeal to lawbreakers.

Because of all of these things, one kidnapping in Philadelphia came to national attention in 1874, when four-year-old Charley Brewster Ross and his six-year-old brother Walter were taken from their home.

Two men in a carriage lured them away with a promise of fireworks. Later they sent Walter into a store to buy the explosives while Charley stayed in the carriage. When Walter came out of the store, the carriage was gone. Although Charley's father received demands for a huge ransom, the boy was never seen again.[1]

Charley Ross's case was the first of a long string of prominent kidnappings that continued for the next half-century, one of which was the notorious abduction and murder of 14-year-old Bobby Franks in 1924 by college students Nathan Leopold and Richard A. Loeb. In 1931 alone, nearly 300 kidnappings took place in America, but juries handed down only 69 kidnapping convictions. By this time the Midwest had become the kidnapping hub of the nation. St. Louis, Missouri, with its good road system and nearness to state borders, saw a particularly bad rash of kidnappings that confounded state officials. Once a kidnapper had taken a victim to another state, the investigation became more complicated, thus giving the kidnappers more time to kill the victim, to get away, or to do both.

For these reasons, the St. Louis Chamber of Commerce, along with the city's mayor, chief of police, and many leading private citizens, organized a committee to seek the passage of a national law that would make kidnapping a federal crime. The committee sought the help of Cleveland A. Newton, a former member of Congress from Missouri, to help bring the matter to Congress's attention. As a result of these efforts, two Missouri members of Congress—Senator Roscoe Conkling Patterson and Representative John Joseph Cochran—introduced kidnapping bills into their respective houses of Congress in 1931.[2]

In each house, the bill was referred to the Judiciary Committee. This referral to committee is a normal part of the lawmaking process. It is also normal for many bills to die in committee—that is, for the committee to take no action on it for one reason or another. This is what happened to each of the kidnapping bills, at least for several months. Then fate intervened, when a high-profile kidnapping suddenly made the issue very important.

Charles A. Lindbergh was one of the most famous men in America. A highly skilled aviator, in 1927 he had flown his custom-designed plane (coincidentally named *The Spirit of St. Louis*) nonstop from New

York to Paris. This first continuous flight from America to Europe cata-pulted Lindbergh to instant fame. Nations bestowed medals upon him, songs were written about him, and one famous dance, the Lindy Hop, was named for him. But not all of the attention he received was good.

In March 1932 Charles A. Lindbergh Jr., the 20-month-old son of Lindbergh and his wife Anne (herself a skilled pilot), was taken from their home in East Amwell, New Jersey. The kidnapper (or kidnappers) left a note demanding $50,000, a huge sum at the time, for the boy's safe return. Because of Lindbergh's fame, the case soon came to national attention. New Jersey and the Lindberghs both offered large rewards for the child's recovery, and numbers of officials and private citizens flocked to help and advise the family. President Herbert Hoover, too, offered his help, although kidnapping was still not a federal crime.

For a month following the kidnapping, the Lindberghs received notes and messages demanding ransom money in exchange for the safe return of "Little Lindy" and warning the parents not to involve the police. In early April, Lindbergh delivered $50,000 to a New York graveyard as he had been instructed to do. He then received a note telling him that the boy was on the boat *Nelly* at Martha's Vineyard in Massachusetts. When Lindbergh arrived there, however, he found no such boat. Then, a month later, the worst happened; the body of the Lindberghs' son was found buried in the woods just a few miles from their home. He had likely been dead since the night of the kidnapping.

In response to the public outcry, the Senate Judiciary Committee and its counterpart in the House of Representatives quickly refocused their attention on the kidnapping bills. Although the bills were iden-tical when first introduced by Senator Patterson and Representative Cochran, each of the two committees now began to rewrite its own bill in different ways. The Senate Judiciary Committee, moved by the wish to encourage kidnappers to return victims unharmed, set the maximum sentence as life imprisonment. Angered at the gravity of the crime, meanwhile, the House Judiciary Committee wrote its version of the bill to make kidnapping punishable by death.

The House committee was also afraid of giving the national govern-ment too much power in an area of criminal law that had always been a matter for state governments to handle. As a result, the House bill left

Charles Lindbergh sits on the witness stand during the trial of Bruno Hauptmann, accused of kidnapping and murdering Lindbergh's son. The kidnapping garnered national attention, which led to the passage of a bill that placed kidnapping under the jurisdiction of federal law enforcement. *AP Photo*

most of the actual kidnapping investigation in the hands of state law officers. Even so, the Chairman of the House committee, John William Summers, had wanted to block the bill's passage altogether because he believed that it allowed the national government to invade the power of the states, but the public furor over the Lindbergh case, and the opposition of other committee members, forced him to back down. As a result, the Judiciary Committee finally reported the amended bill to the House.[3]

Now the entire House of Representatives began debating the revised bill. Some representatives shared the fear of giving the federal government too much power at the expense of the states. Others believed that the only way to investigate kidnappings efficiently was to let federal agents, who could ignore state lines, take the lead. In the end, rather than spending further time in debate, the House agreed to accept the Senate version of the bill, which gave most of the power to investigate kidnappings to federal law enforcement officers. In June 1932, six months after Senator Patterson first introduced the bill and a month after the discovery of "Little Lindy's" body, President Hoover signed it into law. The bill had become a statute, known to this day as the Lindbergh Law.[4]

Over the next two years, federal agents investigated around two dozen kidnappings, prosecuting suspects in nearly all of them and winning a large number of convictions. The number of kidnappings dropped to far lower levels than before, and the conviction rate was much higher. Soon the federal police agency known as the Division of Investigation—soon to be called the Federal Bureau of Investigation, or FBI—had made a lasting name for itself by arresting kidnappers. The Lindbergh Law was a resounding success. In 1934, moreover, Congress amended the law to make it still more effective as well as allowing the death penalty for kidnapping.[5]

The story of the Lindbergh Law reveals the complex process by which a public request for legal change becomes a statute. The rest of this chapter will study in greater detail the legislative process and its role in the criminal law.

The United States has 51 legislatures at the national and state levels: the federal Congress, which is established by the federal Constitution, and 50 state legislatures, each of which is the product of its own state's constitution. In order to pass laws, each of these legislatures must follow a process set forth in the constitution that established it, as well as follow rules of its own making. While these legislatures and rules tend to be very similar, the specifics can differ from legislature to legislature. For instance, Congress and nearly all of the state legislatures are divided into two chambers, or houses (bicameralism), but the Nebraska legislature has only one chamber; for this reason it is informally called the Unicameral (which means "one chamber").

The general process for enacting legislation is similar in most states and in Congress, and is usually set forth by the relevant constitution. A bill must pass each house of the legislature by majority vote and be approved—or at least not vetoed—by the chief executive (the president or the state governor). But the rules that legislatures establish for conducting business and passing laws can be very detailed. Legislative chambers may also have unwritten traditions that its members tend to follow. What seems at first glance to be a straightforward lawmaking process, then, is actually a complex series of steps.

BICAMERALISM

One of the most basic aspects of the legislative process involves the nature of the bicameral system. The two-chamber legislature evolved from the early state governments, which in turn grew out of the colonial practice. In Congress, each state has two senators, each of which serves a six-year term and represents the state as a whole. In the much larger House of Representatives (435 voting members compared to the Senate's 100), a state may have anywhere from one to dozens of representatives, depending on the state's population. Each representative, moreover, typically represents only one geographical part of a state (which is known as a congressional district). Unlike senators, representatives serve only two-year terms. All of these differences mean that the House of Representatives operates differently from the Senate, usually at a faster pace and more along the lines of political party membership. In the Senate, where the fewer number of senators tend to know each other better and serve together longer, the lawmaking process is more deliberate. This means that a law that might pass the House of Representatives easily may meet with more resistance in the Senate, or vice versa.

Another factor that reinforces this difference is the time limit on debate in the House of Representatives. Because of its large size, the House gives each of its members only a short time to speak on each measure. The Senate, however, has no such time limit; each senator may speak as long as he wishes on any subject. Only if 60 senators vote to cut off debate—a vote known as **cloture**—may a senator be silenced. This system allows a combination of 41 or more senators to hold up Senate business indefinitely if they object to a particular bill, simply by refusing to vote for cloture. This stalling tactic is known as a **filibuster** (a Dutch word meaning freebooter or pirate). While actual Senate filibusters are rare, the very possibility of one encourages the majority party in the Senate to work with the minority party more closely than is the case in the House of Representatives, as long as the minority party controls more than 40 seats (which is usually the case). As one scholar has written, "Every member of the Senate has an atomic bomb and can blow up the place. That leads to accommodation."[6] Or, as one senator put it, "One person can tie this place into a knot. . . . And two can do it even more beautifully."[7]

The U.S. House of Representatives' 435 members convene in a special chamber in Washington, D.C. *Brendan Hoffman/Getty Images*

POLITICAL PARTIES AND LEGISLATIVE LEADERSHIP

Although political parties are not mentioned in the original United States Constitution, since the founders did not anticipate their development, they have become a major feature of the American political system. Among other things, political parties have influenced how Congress and the state legislatures operate. Most American legislative chambers have positions of leadership or committee membership that are tied directly to party affiliation.

The leader of the federal House of Representatives, for example, is the Speaker of the House, a position established by the Constitution. Because the Speaker is chosen by vote of the House, and the vote is usually along party lines, the Speaker is always a member of the majority party. The House of Representatives has also established the positions of majority and minority leaders. Each leader is elected by members of his or her party. The majority leader helps the Speaker in scheduling debate and controlling the flow of legislation, while the minority leader works to present alternatives to majority legislation and serves as his or her party's spokesman in the house. Each party also elects a representative to serve as the party whip. A whip's job is to work to turn out the maximum number of votes on issues of importance to the party.[8]

In the United States Senate, the majority and minority leaders have even more power than their counterparts in the House of Representatives. Because the presiding officer of the Senate is the vice president of the United States, who may vote only in order to break a tie, the majority leader has most of the control over scheduling legislation and appointing senators to committees. The senate minority leader is also a powerful figure given the ever-present threat of a filibuster. The Senate, too, has majority and minority whips.

COMMITTEES AND RULES

Political parties also play an important role in committee assignments. Each house in a legislature typically has a number of standing committees, each one focusing on a specific group of related subjects. The chamber's leadership decides which members serve on which committees. Each party normally gets to appoint a number of its members to each committee, although the majority party will always have a majority of members on each committee.

When making committee appointments, the chamber's leaders will rely heavily on a legislator's length of service, or seniority, to decide who serves on the most important committees. New legislators must often serve "apprenticeships" on less important committees before earning the seniority to serve on more prominent ones. Since committees can exercise a great deal of power over bills that come before them, both in terms of what a bill contains and even whether the bill is sent to the chamber for a vote, they play a major role in the legislative process.

In order to conduct business in an orderly way, legislative houses have sets of rules that they must follow. Although in theory a house may vote to change most of these rules at any time, in practice the rules tend to change little over years or decades. (On special occasions a house may vote to suspend the rules temporarily, such as to allow an extended debate on a bill.) Rules may deal with everything from what leadership positions exist to **parliamentary procedure**, the rules governing the introduction of bills, debate, committee referrals, and of course, voting. A legislator who is familiar with the chamber's rules and how to use them can often exercise more power than a legislator with a poor understanding of the rules.

All of these factors—bicameralism, the chief executive's veto power, the role of political parties, the committee system, and legislative rules—mean that the process of lawmaking can be very complex. To understand how all of these things work in practice, it is best to follow the process from beginning to end.

THE PROCESS OF LEGISLATION

A great deal of debate takes place in legislature, both on the floor (that is, in the chamber as a whole) and in committee. Most of this debate is not theoretical; instead, it focuses on actual pieces of proposed legislation, specifically the wording of specific bills. In a sense, the role of a legislature is to examine ideas, as expressed in a bill's wording, and to decide whether to make them into law. The first issue to examine, then, is where these ideas come from.

While legislators may often have general ideas about problems that the law needs to address, other individuals or groups may have a far better understanding of the problem, or perhaps a greater incentive to see that a law is enacted. Sometimes they go so far as to draft a bill that they hope they can get a legislator to introduce.

In the case of the Lindbergh Law, St. Louis citizens and officials were most aware of the need for a federal kidnapping statute. They, in turn, chose Cleveland Newton, a former congressman with good connections in Washington, to encourage Missouri's federal senators and representatives to consider and act on this problem. Newton thus served as a **lobbyist**. Lobbyists are individuals or groups—often paid professionals with good legislative connections—who try to influence the passage or defeat of legislation. The origin of the term lies in the fact that early lobbyists would meet legislators in the lobbies outside the legislative chamber, or in the lobbies of hotels, to discuss the issues that were of importance to them. Today, special interest groups often hire professional lobbyists to pressure legislators to vote a certain way or even to draft bills for legislators to introduce.[9]

A more public source of ideas or bills may be the government employees who must administer the laws that a legislature passes. Corrections officials who are concerned with prison overcrowding, for instance, may ask legislators to change the law on the sentencing of criminals or to fund the construction of more prisons. Chief executives, in particular—that is, governors and presidents—are particularly important sources of ideas for legislation.

While there are many possible sources for ideas and bills, only legislators may actually sponsor a bill, that is, introduce the bill into the legislature for official consideration by his legislative chamber. In the case of the Lindbergh Law, Newton prevailed upon Representative Cochran and Senator Patterson to introduce identical versions of a kidnapping bill into their respective houses of Congress.

Having an influential sponsor, or sponsors, is important, for besides introducing a bill, the sponsor also guides it through the legislative process. A knowledgeable group of sponsors who represent various interest groups or geographic regions, or who serve on the committees through which a bill must pass, can be very helpful in winning the bill's enactment into law.

Once a legislator has a draft bill in hand and decides to sponsor it, he or she must first introduce it. The process of introducing a bill is simple. In the U.S. House of Representatives, for example, the sponsor drops the bill into the hopper, a wooden box located near the front of the chamber. In the federal Senate, a member has the bill printed in the legislative journal known as the *Congressional Record*, or else announces from the floor of the Senate that he is introducing the bill.[11]

The bill's introduction begins the complex process of legislation. Once the bill is introduced, the chamber's presiding officer refers it to the appropriate committee, based on the subject that the bill concerns. In the case of most criminal laws introduced into the federal House of Representatives, the bill goes to the Committee on the Judiciary. The federal Senate also has a Judiciary Committee which, like its counterpart in the House of Representatives, has jurisdiction over bills that involve the criminal law.

The committee's actions regarding the bill are some of the most important steps in the lawmaking process. A committee chairman is likely to exercise a great deal of control over the fate of bills that come before his or her committee. While he or she will usually consult the opinions and wishes of his or her fellow committee members, ultimately he or she has the most influence on the committee. Although committee members who are from the minority party have the least influence they, too, have some input, if only for the reason that some day their party will be in the majority and thus control the committee, and the current majority members will have to work with them. The majority party's desire to avoid alienating the minority party members helps the committee work with a degree of consensus.

A committee may take a number of actions with a bill. On the one hand, it may pigeonhole a bill (a process named after a small coop for a pigeon), putting it out of the way and never bringing it up for discussion. This effectively kills the bill. By refusing to place a bill on the committee's agenda for discussion, the committee leadership can ensure that the bill will not become law. Many bills that are referred to committee, in fact, never go any further. A more dramatic action is for the committee to recommend to the whole chamber that the bill

LEGISLATIVE NOMENCLATURE

As a proposed law moves through a legislature, it may be known by several different names that describe the different stages through which it passes. A **bill**, the most general term, is a proposed new law, or change to an existing law, that the legislature is formally considering. An **amendment** is an alteration made or proposed to be made to a bill. An engrossed bill is a bill that is printed with its amendments included. An enrolled bill is a final copy of a bill that has passed both houses of the legislature and has been prepared for the signatures of the presiding officers of both houses as well as the chief executive (the president or governor). An **act** is a bill that has completed the legislative process by becoming a law. A statute is an act that has been included in a code. A code is a collection of laws organized by subject.

be tabled, or killed; when this happens, the house usually accepts the recommendation.

On the other hand, the chairman may put the bill on the committee's agenda for debate. Another possibility is for the chairman to refer the bill to a subcommittee. A subcommittee, in turn, may hear testimony from expert witnesses on the subject of the bill, or significantly rewrite the bill's language, or seek out compromises between the bill's supporters and opponents. Once the subcommittee has refined and polished the bill, the committee as a whole may then consider it.

During the drafting process, and often while a bill is in committee, lawmakers must decide what sanctions to impose on those who will fail to comply with the new law. The goal of these sanctions, no matter what they are, is to encourage or force compliance with the law. The sanctions, which are usually written directly into the bill, may be civil in nature. For instance, a law specifying that all drivers must have collision insurance may 1) require citizens to show proof of insurance before being permitted to license a car; 2) provide that uninsured motorists are subject to lawsuits by persons they injure; 3) revoke the driver's license of any person found to be driving without insurance; or 4) any combination of these or other sanctions.

A criminal penalty is much harsher than a civil sanction. It places defendants under a cloud and forces them to go to the trouble and expense of a court battle, which is a burden even if they are found to be not guilty. A criminal penalty is also expensive to enforce, since the government must pay at all stages, from police salaries to the costs of prosecution in the courts to the upkeep of prisons. The ideal criminal sanction would dissuade all would-be criminals from breaking the law, but this is an impossible goal. More realistically, a criminal sanction should be harsh enough to convince citizens not to commit the crime, but not so harsh as to make judges and juries reluctant to convict those accused of the crime. In theory, a legislature could establish the death penalty for all criminal offenses, including double-parking and jaywalking, but such stern measures could never be enforced. In that case, the laws against such behavior would be useless. When drafting criminal statutes, then, legislators must strike a balance when deciding on criminal as well as civil sanctions.[12]

Because of the committee system, legislators tend to know more about the subjects that their committees deal with than they do about other areas of law. Likewise, when a bill is in committee, the members of that committee become more familiar with it than their fellow lawmakers. This, in turn, means that a committee's recommendation to a chamber about what to do with a bill that has been assigned to it carries a great deal of weight. If a committee reports a bill favorably to the whole house, then the house is likely to follow the recommendation. For these reasons, lobbying efforts often focus heavily on committees.

When the committee has finished with the bill and finds it satisfactory, it reports the bill favorably back to the chamber as a whole. (Remember, however, that many bills die in committee.) This is perhaps the major hurdle that a bill faces after its introduction. But some hurdles still remain.

Opponents of a bill may move to re-refer the bill to committee, either the original one or another committee that has a claim to jurisdiction over the bill's subject matter. A motion to re-refer is an effort to make the bill clear the hurdle of committee recommendation all over again, so re-referral is a major setback. Even if the motion to re-refer fails, the bill must compete with many other bills for the chamber's limited amount of time. For this reason it must win a favored spot on the chamber's legislative calendar or else risk dying if the chamber adjourns without voting on it. In the U.S. House of Representatives, major bills that have been reported favorably by their committees must then go before the Rules Committee, which assigns each of them a priority for consideration. The higher a bill's priority, the sooner the House will consider the bill. This makes the Rules Committee a very powerful one and an important agency in deciding which bills become law.[12]

Ultimately, to win passage into law, a bill must be approved by a majority of those legislators who are present and voting, or in some legislatures by a majority of all the members, present or not. Voting may take place in several ways; the most common are the voice vote, in which all of the bill's supporters simultaneously say "Aye" and all opponents then simultaneously say "No," and the recorded vote. Unlike the voice vote, the recorded vote is a way of creating a formal record of how each legislator has voted on the bill. In smaller chambers, the recorded vote may take place by roll call, while in larger houses, the recorded vote may take place in other ways, particularly in modern times with the help of an electronic system.[13] Even when the bill has been approved, however, it must still win approval from the other house of the legislature.

Passage in the second chamber is usually easier than passage in the original house. The original committee that considered the bill in the first house is likely to have done most of polishing and political "horse-trading" necessary to make it acceptable to a variety of interests, so it will need less adjustment during its consideration by the other house. Members of the second house are also likely to assume that the bill has considerable merit; otherwise, their reasoning goes, the first house would not have passed it. Nevertheless, the second house will still follow most of the same committee and voting procedures as the first house did in considering the bill, allowing for any structural differences in how the two houses operate.

If the second house approves the same identical bill as the first house, then the bill is ready for the signature of the chief executive. But if the second house has amended the bill—that is, changed it in any way—before approving it, then the first house must agree by majority vote to all of the changes. This is an absolute requirement, since otherwise each house would essentially have passed different bills, thus defeating the whole point of bicameralism.

Sometimes the two houses cannot agree on any amendments that have occurred. In this case they must create a **conference committee** if the bill is to become a law. A conference committee consists of members from each of the two houses, and it has the job of hammering out the disagreements between the two chambers and the differences between the two versions of the bill. Although the committee may be formally limited as to what changes it can make, in practice it may go further, since by this point the entire legislature has invested a great deal of time and energy on the bill and will be reluctant to defeat it even if the conference committee changes it significantly, and the committee members know this.[14]

Finally, when the same version of a bill has won the approval of both houses, it is ready for the signature of the chief executive (the governor at the state level and the president at the national level). Under the federal Constitution, which has a typical process for executive approval

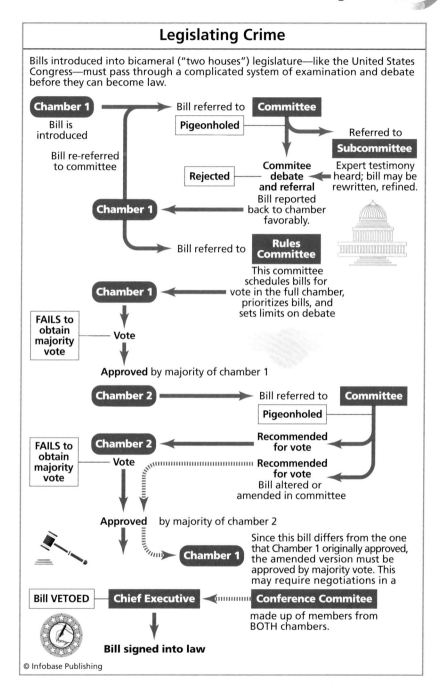

Legislating Crime

Bills introduced into bicameral ("two houses") legislature—like the United States Congress—must pass through a complicated system of examination and debate before they can become law.

Chamber 1
Bill is introduced

Bill re-referred to committee

Bill referred to **Committee**

Pigeonholed

Referred to **Subcommittee**
Expert testimony heard; bill may be rewritten, refined.

Commitee debate and referral ← Rejected

Chamber 1 ← Bill reported back to chamber favorably.

Bill referred to **Rules Committee**
This committee schedules bills for vote in the full chamber, prioritizes bills, and sets limits on debate

Chamber 1

FAILS to obtain majority vote — Vote

Approved by majority of chamber 1

Chamber 2 → Bill referred to **Committee**

Pigeonholed

Recommended for vote

FAILS to obtain majority vote — **Chamber 2**

Vote — **Recommended for vote**
Bill altered or amended in committee

Approved by majority of chamber 2

Chamber 1
Since this bill differs from the one that Chamber 1 originally approved, the amended version must be approved by majority vote. This may require negotiations in a

Bill VETOED — **Chief Executive** ← **Conference Commitee**
made up of members from BOTH chambers.

Bill signed into law

© Infobase Publishing

of a law, the president may sign the bill, veto it, or take no action upon it. If he or she signs it, it becomes an act—a law. If he or she vetoes, or rejects it, he or she returns it to Congress with a statement of his or her objections to it. In this case the bill has not passed into law. Vetoes, while somewhat uncommon, are by no means unknown. But if the president does veto a bill, Congress may vote on it once again. If two-thirds of the members of each house vote in favor of it, the bill becomes law despite the president's veto. This is known as an **override**. Overrides are rare; out of nearly 1,500 presidential vetoes to occur from the years 1789 to 2000, Congress only voted to override about 100 of them. But when an override occurs, it is usually a major political setback for the president.[15]

If the president takes no action on a bill, two results are possible. If Congress is still in session 10 days after it has transmitted a bill to the president, it becomes law without his or her signature. But if Congress adjourns before the 10 days have elapsed, the lawmaking process for that bill has been interrupted before its completion, and the bill fails to become law. This is known as a **pocket veto**. At the federal level, about 1,000 pocket vetoes occurred from 1789 to the year 2000.[16]

In the last century, legislation has become an increasingly important source of the criminal law, but the common law continues to be highly important as well.

5

The Elements of Criminal Law

George M. "Mart" Rider was a dangerous man living in a dangerous place and time. In the 1880s Saline County, Missouri, was still rough-and-tumble, and its citizens still remembered the Civil War, when both the Union and the Confederacy claimed the state for their own, and family had fought against family. Rider's own father may have been the Confederate guerilla who had ridden with the notorious raider William Quantrill, and Rider himself was a man with a violent temper. In 1883, using a club, he savagely beat Mary Moore, the woman with whom he was living. Moore, who sometimes went by the name of Mary Rider and whom Rider claimed to be his wife, then fled to the home of R. P. Tallent and his wife for protection. ("She was as bloody as a hog," Mrs. Tallent later declared.) Moore told Mrs. Tallent that she was afraid that Rider would kill her.

R. P. Tallent took Mary Moore away from Saline County for a while, and when the two returned, they had begun a relationship—one that made Mart Rider both jealous and furious. Soon Rider and Tallent were deadly enemies, and more than once in the next year or two, Tallent threatened to kill Rider.

On July 23, 1885, the showdown came. Mary Moore again went to the Tallents, telling Mrs. Tallent once more that she feared that Mart Rider was going to kill her. R. P. Tallent then rowed Moore across the Missouri River to the neighboring village of Brunswick. But by the time he returned, Mart Rider was looking for him.

When Rider learned that Moore was missing, he decided that she must be with the Tallents. As dusk fell, Rider armed himself with a shotgun, but that was not enough. On the way to the Tallents' home, he came across Milton Campbell while on the road and took Campbell's pistol at gunpoint.

It was after nightfall when Rider arrived at the Tallent place. Starting down the path to the river, Rider came upon Tallent himself, who was wielding an axe. Holding his shotgun, Rider demanded to know where Mary Moore was.

"I have taken her where you won't find her," said Tallent. "Damn you, we might as well settle this right here." With that he hefted his axe and started toward Rider.

Rider ordered Tallent to stop, but the other man kept coming. Rider then fired the shotgun. One shot was all he needed.

Tallent staggered down the path to his home. Encountering his wife, he cried out. "Oh hun," he exclaimed, "he has shot me!" Before long Tallent lay dead.

Immediately after the fight, Rider told a friend of his that he had had to shoot Tallent, who had been coming at him with an axe. But the story did not stop a grand jury from indicting Rider for murder.

No one saw the fight except Rider and Tallent, but everyone knew of the bad blood between the two men. Everyone remembered what Mary Moore had looked like when Rider had finished with her. But everyone also knew that she had gotten involved with Tallent and that Tallent himself had threatened to kill Rider at least twice. Tallent's axe was riddled with shot, so it was clear that he had been holding it when Rider gunned him down. Still, in light of all of this evidence, a jury found Mart Rider guilty of murder, and he appealed to Missouri's Supreme Court.

Rider's argument was simple. Even though he had been armed with a shotgun and pistol, Tallent had attacked first. Rider had merely been defending himself. Things did look bad for him on the surface: He had gone onto Tallent's land, armed with two weapons, to look for Tallent. But Rider argued that because Tallent had attacked first, whatever Rider had planned did not matter, for instead of acting on his own plan to kill Tallent, he was merely defending himself from *Tallent's* attack.

The Missouri Supreme Court agreed with Rider and reversed his conviction. There was plenty of evidence to suggest that Tallent had been the one to start the fight that night. And if that was the case, then Rider was not guilty of murder.[1]

Rider seemed to want to kill Tallent, and he did kill Tallent. So why did the Supreme Court throw out the murder conviction? The answer reveals a great deal about the elements of a crime—any crime.

A few hypothetical situations will help explain the *Rider* case. Suppose that Debbie wants to kill Jason. She drives to Jason's home and knocks on the door. When Jason opens the door, Debbie stabs and kills him. This would seem to be a clear case of murder. Likewise, suppose that Debbie, wanting to kill Jason, sees Jason on the sidewalk and deliberately runs over him. Again, this clearly seems to be murder.

Compare this to the case of Edwin and Wendy. As Edwin is driving down the street, he swerves to avoid Jo, a police officer who has run into his path while chasing a fugitive. But when Edwin swerves he runs over and kills his good friend Wendy, whom he of course did not want to kill. This is clearly not a case of murder, even though it is still a **homicide** (a term used for any situation in which one person kills another).

What is different in these two cases? In each situation, the killer's actions caused the victim's death. The difference is in the two killers' intentions, or states of mind. Debbie wanted to kill Jason; Edwin did not want to kill Wendy.

Now consider another case. Laura hates Marc and wants him to die. Laura never stops hating Marc. Laura lives 50 more years, wishing every day for Marc's death. But Laura never tries in any way to bring about Marc's death, and when Laura dies of old age, Marc is still alive.

Obviously Laura has not murdered Marc. In fact, Laura has committed no crime at all. Laura's situation is the exact opposite of Edwin's. Edwin's actions killed Wendy, but Edwin did not wish Wendy's death. Laura, on the other hand, wished Marc's death but never committed any action that killed Marc.

Finally, consider the case of Maggy and Stephen. Maggy hates Stephen and wants to kill him, just as Laura hated Marc. Maggy buys a gun with which to shoot Stephen, but then she changes her mind and decides not to go through with the crime. Unlike Laura and Marc, Maggy and

Stephen work out their differences and become friends. But the following week, Maggy accidentally runs over Stephen and kills him.

Most people would say that Maggy has not murdered Stephen. But Maggy, like Debbie, had the wish (or in legal terms, the **intent**) to kill her victim, and also like Debbie, Maggy's actions did kill her victim. How, then, is Maggy different from Debbie?

The difference is that with Maggy, as with Mart Rider, the intent to kill her victim and the act of killing him were unrelated. In legal terms, Maggy's intent to kill Stephen did not cause the action of Maggy that in turn caused Stephen's death. Likewise, Rider's initial wish to kill Tallent was unconnected to his actual killing of Tallent in self-defense.

These cases illustrate some of the most basic and most important things about the elements of criminal law. First, to be guilty of criminal conduct, a person must have a criminal state of mind, also known as *mens rea*, or "guilty mind." Second, to be guilty of criminal conduct, one must commit a criminal act, known in Latin as *actus reus*, or "guilty act." Third, the criminal state of mind must cause the criminal act.[2]

MENS REA

It is obvious that different actions may lead to different crimes. The act of killing a person is homicide; the act of robbing a bank is not. But less obvious is that just as a person can commit different criminal acts, so, too, a person can have different criminal states of mind.

For instance, compare the circumstances of two drivers, Posey and Olivia. Posey wishes to kill Raymond. She sees Raymond crossing the street in front of her and deliberately runs over and kills him. Posey has committed the homicide known as murder.

Olivia, on the other hand, wishes to kill no one. Nevertheless, she drives her car at 100 miles an hour down a crowded street while trying to dodge all of the pedestrians, knowing that her actions are very dangerous. But she fails to miss Justin and kills him.

Olivia did not have any intent to kill Justin or anyone else, but she was behaving in a way that she knew was endangering other peoples' lives. This fact makes her responsible for Justin's death. Typically, depending on the law of the state where this crime occurs, Olivia will be guilty of **manslaughter**—a type of criminal homicide that, while serious, is punished to a lesser degree than murder. The point here is that the actions of Posey and Olivia, or at least the results of those actions, are the same: each drove a car in such a way as to kill someone. The difference lies only in their mental states or *mens rea*. While both mental states are criminal, their different degrees of *mens rea* mean that the two drivers are guilty of different crimes.

The Model Penal Code sets forth five different levels of *mens rea*. The highest level is **intent**, the purpose to do a forbidden act or cause a forbidden result. The next level is **knowledge** about the nature of an act or the results that an act is likely to cause (as was the case with Olivia). In some states, knowledge might even be enough to charge a defendant with murder, although in others knowledge might only be enough for manslaughter.[3]

The third level is **recklessness**. This level is similar to the knowledge level in that the person committing the act in question knows that his or her actions might produce a bad result. The difference is one of likelihood. For instance, look more closely at Olivia, the high-speed driver. If the street she is traveling has a very crowded intersection, she will

COMMON LAW INTENT

The Model Penal Code's approach to criminal mental states is fairly new. Many states still follow the common law approach. Because so many courts have been involved over the centuries in developing this approach, sometimes the language can be confusing, and the exact meaning of terms can vary from state to state. Criminal intent, for instance, can mean not only intent in the Model Penal Code sense, but also knowledge, recklessness, and negligence. General intent normally means an intention to do an act, while specific intent is an intent *more* than just to do an act. For instance, to prove that Ben is guilty of larceny under the common law, a prosecutor must show not only that Ben intentionally took Jerry's property; she must also prove that when Ben did so, he specifically intended to steal that property when he took it.

meet the knowledge level of *mens rea*, because she knows that there is an excellent chance that she will hit someone. But if she is instead driving down a road with little traffic and few pedestrians, then she will meet only the recklessness level. It is not very likely that a pedestrian will walk in front of her car on this street—but if it does happen, Olivia knows that she will hit him. Recklessness is typically not enough for murder but is sufficient to convict a defendant of manslaughter.

The fourth level is that of **negligence**. In one way negligence is somewhat like recklessness. In each situation, the person is doing something that he or she knows is creating a risk of harm. But with negligence, the risk may be even lower than is the case with recklessness, or perhaps the social benefit of the action is higher. If Olivia is driving at such high speeds because she is running late to work she is probably reckless, but if she is rushing her gravely ill brother to the hospital, this may reduce her state of mind from the reckless level to the negligence level.

The most important difference in recklessness and negligence, however, is that with recklessness a person *must actually realize* that he or she is creating a danger. But a person may be charged with negligence not only when he or she knows that his or her actions are dangerous but when he or she *should have known* that his or her actions are dangerous. The law often states that a defendant is negligent when a *reasonable person* in his or her position would know he or she was being negligent. This usually makes negligence easier to prove than recklessness, or for that matter knowledge and intent. On the other hand, negligence is not a mental state serious enough to convict a defendant of more serious crimes.[4]

The fifth and final mental state is a special case, involving a crime that carries **liability without fault**. The most common example of this is the **strict liability crime**. In a crime of this sort, the defendant does not need to have any criminal mental state at all; he or she merely has to commit the criminal act. An example might include parking next to a fire hydrant. If the legislature makes this a strict liability crime, then the driver does not even need to know that he or she has parked next to it, and the state does not even need to prove that the driver should have known that he or she had parked next to it. It is enough that the driver has parked there. Another example of liability without fault is vicarious liability, in which the law makes one person liable for another person's fault, such as an employer being penalized for the acts of his or her employee, or parents being penalized for the acts of their young children.

The notion of liability without fault flies in the face of the centuries-old idea that to be guilty of a crime the defendant must have *mens rea*, that is, a criminal mental state. For this reason, strict liability and vicarious liability crimes are a very narrow exception to this rule. They carry only very small penalties (usually the payment of a small fine, and never imprisonment) and seek to regulate a widespread type of behavior in which proving defendants' mental states would be hard to do.[5]

It is important to remember that liability without fault is the exception in criminal law. The great majority of criminal offenses—and all major crimes—require proof of some level of *mens rea*.

ACTUS REUS

The idea of the criminal act, like that of *mens rea*, is more complex than it first appears. Generally, "act" means some sort of physical motion as opposed to the bad state of mind that makes up *mens rea*. But not all physical acts that produce bad results will make the defendant criminally liable even when coupled with *mens rea*, and there may be situations when a person is criminally liable because he or she has *failed* to act. This failure is known as an **omission**.

Some cases are easy ones. If Robert picks up a gun and aims at and shoots Trevor, the action is clear: It is the picking up, aiming, and firing of the gun. But what if Robert is a sleepwalker and he shoots Trevor while Robert is actually asleep? (There really have been cases like this.)[6] Even if Robert hates Trevor, if Robert's action is involuntary—the result of a reflex, or convulsions, or something similar—then the necessary connection between the bad action and the bad mental state does not exist. There are many such examples in real life. Imagine a situation in which public drunkenness is illegal. Police officers raid Peg's house, suspecting that she has murdered Tommy. They find Peg, who is drunk, inside her house, and they arrest her and take her outside to a waiting police car. While outside, Peg is in public, but she has not appeared in public voluntarily, so she is not guilty of public drunkenness.[7]

This raises another issue. An act does not need to be a single physical movement, such as pulling a trigger, or even a group of related movements, such as Robert's picking up, aiming, and firing a gun. An act can be, like Peg's public drunkenness, an ongoing set of circumstances. An example is the crime of knowingly possessing illegal drugs. Suppose that Carol sells Lorraine a package of white powder that Lorraine believes is talcum or flour. Lorraine is not guilty of this crime because she does not know (as this law requires) that the powder is really cocaine. But the next day Lorraine learns that the powder is in fact cocaine. At that point she becomes criminally liable without any new physical action on her part, because her possession is a sort of ongoing act. Only her state of mind has changed.

Someone can also become guilty of a crime by the act of speaking (if coupled, of course, with a criminal mental state). Suppose that Steve is on trial for murdering Barry. Julie, a witness, testifies in court under oath that she saw Steve stab Barry to death. Based on Julie's testimony, the jury finds Steve guilty and the judge sentences Steve to death. But as it turns out, Julie was lying because she hates Steve and wants him to die. This makes Julie guilty of the crime of perjury, or lying under oath. Because Julie's lie resulted in Steve's execution, Julie, by the mere act of speaking (coupled with her *mens rea*) has murdered Steve. So, too, if Phillip, a mobster, orders Warren, a hit man, to kill Gwen, and Warren does so, Phillip's orders can make him guilty (along with Warren) of Gwen's murder. Even an agreement between Phillip and Warren to commit the murder, without it actually being completed, can make them guilty of the crime of **conspiracy** to commit murder as long as they had taken some substantial step toward killing Gwen. If Phillip and Warren had agreed to burn down a warehouse instead and taken substantial steps to do so, they are guilty of the crime of conspiracy to commit arson.[8]

One of the most interesting and important issues regarding *actus reus* is when *failure* to act makes a person liable. The law always requires a criminal act, but oddly enough, this can sometimes mean an absence of physical action.

Suppose that a mother knows that her child is dying of pneumonia, but she does not call a doctor or take her child to a hospital. If the child dies, the mother may be guilty of murder, or at least some other criminal degree of homicide. Or suppose that a law requires all citizens to file an income tax return and a citizen fails to do so. By this failure to act, he or she has violated the law.

Making people liable for failing to act creates a danger of expanding the criminal law far beyond what could be enforced. Imagine, for instance, that a driver has a flat tire on the bridge of a very busy interstate highway during a rainy night. Dozens, perhaps hundreds, of motorists drive by and see him in the bridge's emergency lane, but none stops to pick him up or help him change the tire. As a result, he is run over and killed a few minutes later. Should we charge all of the drivers who passed by him with negligent homicide? Perhaps morally they are to blame, but even if they are, how would we even find them all? What if they were afraid for their own lives if they stopped in such dangerous conditions? What if stopping would have only increased the danger to everyone passing over the bridge? This shows some of the problems involved in having too many situations in which a failure to act is illegal.

A harder case is when only a few people are involved. Suppose that someone is drowning in a lake or at the seashore. An Olympic gold medalist swimmer stands on the beach watching. Is she guilty of homicide if she refuses to swim out and rescue the drowning man? Most courts would say that she is not. What if a lifeguard is on duty and standing next to the Olympic medalist? The lifeguard's job is to make sure that swimmers on that beach are safe. For this reason, if the lifeguard fails to try to rescue the drowning swimmer, then in most states the lifeguard *would* be guilty of homicide.

Why does the law treat the medalist and the lifeguard differently? The distinction is that the lifeguard is under a legal duty to try to help the swimmer, and because of the difficulty of enforcement, the law finds that such a duty exists only in certain situations. One such situation in which courts have found such a duty is when the victim and the defendant have some special family, legal, or contractual relationship to each other, such as parent and child or husband and wife, two drivers involved in an accident, or a bodyguard or lifeguard. If someone owns land on which a dangerous condition exists, or if someone has created a danger that did not exist before, or is in charge of small children who may, if not controlled, pose a danger to others by their behavior, then he or she generally has a duty to act to keep others safe from the danger. Further, if someone who originally had no duty to the victim (such as our Olympic medalist) begins to try to aid a victim, the law may require her to follow through with the help, since by starting to give assistance she may have made others decide not to help, thus leaving the victim in a worse position.[9]

CAUSATION

Even if someone with a criminal mental state acts in a criminal way, and the mental state is connected to the criminal act, something else is needed for guilt: This criminal conduct must cause a criminal result. For instance, if Allan, wanting to kill Sue, shoots at Sue and misses her, Allan is not guilty of homicide because he has not caused the result needed for the crime of homicide (namely, someone's death). Normally this question of **causation**, or the link between the defendant's mental state and actions on the one hand and the criminal result on the other, is an easy one, but sometimes difficult cases arise. The two big issues of causation are **cause in fact** and **legal cause**, also known as **proximate cause**. Both cause in fact and proximate cause must be present for the defendant to be guilty of crime.

Cause in Fact

Suppose that Larry engages in criminal conduct and that Maureen then dies. Traditionally, in deciding whether cause in fact exists, courts have asked the following question: "Would Maureen still have died even if Larry had not done what he did?" If the answer is "yes," then Larry is not guilty because his conduct did not cause Maureen's death.

The problem here arises when there is more than one possible cause. Suppose that during a riot, and at the same instant, Tim and Donna both hit Jenny with clubs or rocks hard enough to kill her. The medical examiner conducts an autopsy and finds that Jenny would have died from either blow by itself. In other words, Jenny would still have died from Donna's blow if Tim had not struck her, and Jenny would still have died from Tim's blow if Donna had not struck her. Does this mean that *neither* attacker should be found guilty of killing Jenny?

A similar situation is when Phil wants to burn down Vicki's house and starts a fire nearby. But at the same time lightning starts another fire, and both fires reach Vicki's house at the same time. The second fire would have burned down the house even if Phil had not set his fire. Does this mean that because of the lightning strike Phil is innocent?

In cases like these, courts have often found that cause in fact does exist—that is, that persons such as Tim, Donna, and Phil are guilty—because their conduct amounted to substantial factors in the bad result. Nevertheless, these cases remain troubling and have led different courts to reach different decisions.[10]

Proximate Cause

The question of legal, or proximate, cause is even more complicated. Suppose that Clint, wanting to kill Susan, shoots and injures her. With medical treatment, Susan would normally survive. But what if a gas main in the hospital explodes a few days later near the room where Susan is recuperating and kills her?

Some people would argue that in this case Clint is still liable for Susan's death since he put her in the position in which she was killed by the explosion (although many courts disagree). But if we hold Clint responsible in this case, then how far should we stretch this argument? Suppose that Susan is a world-famous surgeon and that when Clint shot her she was on the way to perform a major operation on Sally. Because Susan was not available to operate on Sally that day, Sally's condition grows worse and she dies a month later, even though a less-skilled doctor tried to save her. Is Clint also guilty of killing Sally, whom he does not even know? Suppose in turn that Sally is a police officer, and because she died no policeman is available six months later to prevent a bank robbery in which Mona, a bank teller, is stabbed to death. Is Clint guilty of causing Mona's death? Most courts would say that Clint is not guilty of the deaths of Sally or Mona, because their deaths, in terms of causation, are not connected closely (or proximately) enough to Clint's criminal conduct towards Susan.

On the other hand, what if Clint shoots at Susan just as she is wheeling Sally into the operating room, misses Susan, but hits and kills Sally instead? Here most courts *would* find Clint guilty of murder, even though Clint did not intend to harm Sally at all. The reason is that Clint did intend to shoot and kill someone, and someone was shot and killed. The bad result here is causally much more closely related to the bad conduct.[11]

The issue of proximate cause is a very difficult one. In fact, it is one of the most complicated aspects of the criminal law, occupying some of the best legal minds.

JUSTIFICATION, EXCUSE, AND CAPACITY

In some cases, all of the elements of a crime may be present (including *mens rea*, *actus reus*, causation, and bad result), yet the defendant is still not guilty of the crime. This is because the circumstances justify or excuse his or her conduct. In other cases the elements of the crime all appear to be present, but the defendant may rely on some well-accepted theory to show that he or she must have lacked *mens rea* and so could not have committed the crime, or in legal terms, that he or she lacked the *capacity* to commit the crime. There are several types of justification. One of the most famous types occurred in the *Rider* case: the justification of self-defense.

Self-Defense

When Mart Rider killed R. P. Tallent, he clearly had the intent to do so, but only because Tallent had attacked him first. His killing of Tallent, rather than being connected to his original intention to murder Tallent, was instead linked only to his wish to defend himself from Tallent's attack. In such cases, the law allows a person to use enough force to defend himself from an immediate threat of death or grave harm. Likewise, someone may use force to defend a third person from such an attack, or even to protect his property from damage or destruction (although in the case of protection of property, a person generally may not use deadly force). The idea behind self-defense is that the person defending him or herself is only doing for him or herself what the law would normally do, and that it is better that the attacker than the victim suffer injury.[12] This leads to the second main justification.

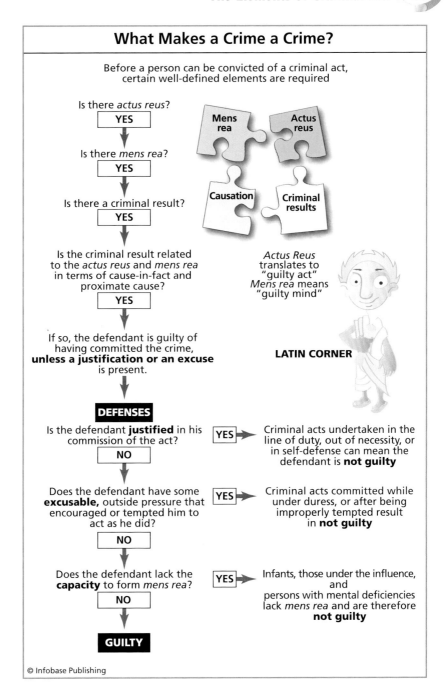

What Makes a Crime a Crime?

Before a person can be convicted of a criminal act, certain well-defined elements are required

Is there *actus reus*?
YES

Is there *mens rea*?
YES

Is there a criminal result?
YES

Is the criminal result related to the *actus reus* and *mens rea* in terms of cause-in-fact and proximate cause?
YES

If so, the defendant is guilty of having committed the crime, **unless a justification or an excuse** is present.

DEFENSES

Is the defendant **justified** in his commission of the act? **YES** ➤ Criminal acts undertaken in the line of duty, out of necessity, or in self-defense can mean the defendant is **not guilty**
NO

Does the defendant have some **excusable,** outside pressure that encouraged or tempted him to act as he did? **YES** ➤ Criminal acts committed while under duress, or after being improperly tempted result in **not guilty**
NO

Does the defendant lack the **capacity** to form *mens rea*? **YES** ➤ Infants, those under the influence, and persons with mental deficiencies lack *mens rea* and are therefore **not guilty**
NO

GUILTY

Mens rea   **Actus reus**

Causation   **Criminal results**

Actus Reus translates to "guilty act"
Mens rea means "guilty mind"

LATIN CORNER

© Infobase Publishing

Public Duty

The classic example of this defense is that of a police officer who must use force to defend him or herself or others, or to make an arrest, or to

enforce the law in some other way. Another example is that of a fire-
man who must destroy property, such as kicking down a door, in order
to fight a fire that is threatening even more property. When the public
officer faces only a choice between two evils, the law encourages him to
choose the lesser of them by holding him or her free of blame for it.[13]

Necessity

The *Dudley* case involved this defense. The basic element of necessity is
an immediate threat from some natural force or circumstance. If Jim is
lost in the woods and starving to death, the law allows him to take food
from Cindy's empty cabin to save his life. (Because Dudley and Stephens
ate not Parker's food but Parker himself, their actions were much more
serious, especially since there was also a question as to whether the threat
of starvation was immediate enough.) Likewise, when a prisoner escapes
from a burning jail in order to keep from dying in the fire, the law will not
hold him or her guilty of jail breaking. Again, with the necessity defense,
the law permits the person to choose the lesser of the two evils.[14]

Duress

This justification is somewhat similar to necessity in that the defendant
is acting because of some sort of understandable pressure. But while in
necessity cases the pressure comes from circumstances, in the case of
duress it comes from another person. For instance, if Phillip, a gangster,
threatens to kill Stephanie's husband, David, unless Stephanie robs a
bank for Phillip, then Stephanie may use the defense of duress if she is
tried for robbing the bank.[15]

Entrapment

With necessity, and even more with duress, the defendant's free will
seems compromised or limited in some way, but *mens rea* still exists.
The starving woodsman Jim intentionally kicks in Cindy's cabin door
and steals the food he finds there; Stephanie intentionally enters a bank,
aims a gun at a teller, and demands money. With entrapment, too, *mens
rea* still exists, but the person's will is even more impaired.

    If a mobster bribes a politician, the bribery is usually secret and
therefore hard or impossible to prove, even if the police suspect that

it has happened. As part of their investigation, they may have an undercover agent try to bribe the politician again. If the politician falls for the ruse and takes the money, promising to vote as the agent directs, then the police have enough evidence to make an arrest for this second instance of bribery (but not the first). But if the police had not approached the politician to begin with, the crime of which he is accused would not even have occurred. This is the idea behind the entrapment defense.

Because this sort of police encouragement to commit a crime is often the only way to capture persons suspected of crimes that take place between willing participants (such as bribery, gambling, or drug dealing), the courts often allow it. With entrapment, the issue is whether such encouragement has gone too far. Generally the line seems to be **predisposition**: Was the defendant already predisposed to commit the crime by the time law officers approached him? A politician who accepts bribe money after only one or two meetings with an agent is much less likely to win with an entrapment defense than one who resisted a number of bribery offers over several years before finally giving in. Still, the exact line is hard to draw.[16]

Mistake or Ignorance

This is the final type of justification, and it is one of the most famous. Of all of the justifications, this one goes the furthest toward actually eliminating the *mens rea* element altogether, thus showing that with mistake (unlike the previous defenses) a needed element of the crime was absent to begin with.

Suppose a statute declares that a person who knowingly takes another's property is guilty of theft. Scotty, leaving a restaurant on a rainy night, picks up an umbrella that she thinks is hers, but which actually belongs to Tommy. Is Scotty guilty of theft? No, because she has not *knowingly* taken Tommy's property. In other words, her mistake about who owned the umbrella means that she lacked the needed *mens rea*. This was a mistake of fact—the fact of who owned the umbrella.

What if Scotty *did* know that the umbrella belonged to Tommy and took it anyway, but she believed that there was no law against the taking of umbrellas? Is Scotty guilty now? Yes, because she did have the mental state, and committed the act, that the statute sets forth. Scotty is still mistaken, but this time her mistake has no effect on her mental state of knowingly taking the umbrella. This is a case in which the famous saying "ignorance of the law is no excuse" applies.[17]

Actually, however, even ignorance of the law can be an excuse, just as a mistake of fact can be an excuse, if the ignorance or mistake means that the defendant lacked *mens rea*. Suppose that a state has a law against bigamy, or the practice of having more than one spouse at the same time. Henry, who believes that a court order in his possession is a divorce decree ending his marriage to Katherine, his wife, then marries another woman, Anne. But the court order was actually not a final divorce decree, and so Henry is still married to Katherine. Henry is mistaken about the law (the meaning of the court order) and his mistake means that he lacked the *mens rea* to commit bigamy. (In fact, something very much like this happened to General Andrew Jackson several years before he became president of the United States. He apparently married Rachel Donelson Robards in 1791 after hearing that she had been granted a divorce, but it later turned out that the divorce had never become official. The couple married again after taking steps to finalize the divorce.)[18]

The defense of mistake has been a very confusing one in the criminal law, largely because of the false distinction between mistakes of fact and mistakes of law. In reality, the defense is very simple: If a defendant's mistake means that he or she does not have the *mens rea* needed to commit the crime, then he or she has not committed the crime.

Responsibility

The first defenses examined involved situations in which the defendants freely chose to engage in conduct that is normally criminal, but which the law allowed in their particular circumstances. The second type of defenses involved situations in which the defendants, while still freely choosing to commit the acts they did, were under some excusable outside pressure that encouraged or tempted them to act as they did. The mistake defense involved cases in which the defendants had actually not formed a criminal state of mind at all, and so had not committed any crime to begin with. The final type of defense includes situations in which the defendant is *unable* to have *mens rea*. In legal terms, such persons lack responsibility, or the **capacity** to commit the crimes of which they are accused.

IGNORANCE OF THE LAW

A famous saying declares that "Ignorance of the law is no excuse." This means, for instance, that if Charlotte robs a bank and does not know that bank robbery is a crime, then Charlotte is still guilty of the crime of bank robbery. But why should this be so, especially in modern America with its huge number of criminal laws, where no one is able to know every possible criminal offense?

One argument is that if ignorance of the law were an excuse, then every criminal defendant could claim that he or she did not know that his or her actions were illegal, thus slowing trials and tying up courts so badly that the criminal justice system would break down. Juries would also have to investigate whether a defendant *should have known* about the law he or she allegedly broke, which would add another level of difficulty to trials. Another argument is that the law is the command of the community that is binding upon all members of society; the law is not what individual members of society believe it to be. By allowing defendants to decide what the law is by their own ignorance, the legal system would be destroying its own authority. Still another reason is that the very act of prosecuting and punishing someone for breaking a law he or she did not know about will help educate other members of society about the existence of that law.

Nevertheless, punishing individuals for breaking laws they honestly did not know about and had no reason to know about has struck many people as harsh. This difficulty is one reason why police and prosecutors have some discretion in deciding who to charge for crimes. If charging someone for an honest mistake about the law when his or her conduct is not dangerous to the community would be unjust, then police and prosecutors may choose to warn the wrongdoer and release him or her instead.

Infancy

Traditionally, children under the age of seven have been held to lack the ability to form criminal states of mind. The notion behind this is that such young children cannot understand the meaning of what they are doing. Punishing them for doing something they cannot understand would not deter others from engaging in the same conduct, since adults would not identify with the children who were being punished, and other young children would be unable to do so either.

From age seven to 14, children are also presumed not to have the capacity to form *mens rea*, but with this age group prosecutors may introduce evidence to show otherwise. For instance, if a 10-year-old not only shot and killed his father but also hid the body, this concealment may show that the child did understand that his act was wrong.

All states now have special courts for children, known as **juvenile courts**, which have different rules than regular courts. The juvenile system is discussed in another section.[19]

Intoxication

Being under the influence of alcohol, or of any other mind-altering drug, may mean that the defendant cannot think clearly enough to form some types of criminal states of mind. If Laura attacks Marc, but Laura is too intoxicated to form an intent to kill Marc, then Laura cannot be guilty of the crime of assault with intent to kill.

While intoxication may mean that the defendant does not have the ability to reach the "intent" and "knowledge" levels of *mens rea*, the law normally finds that he or she may still reach the "recklessness" and "negligence" levels. Negligence holds a defendant not only to what he or she knows but to what a reasonable person knows, and intoxication does not change this standard. (One might say that a reasonable person would not be intoxicated.) Likewise, in the case of recklessness, many courts hold that using mind-altering drugs to the point of intoxication is in itself reckless behavior that makes a person liable for the reckless acts he or she commits while intoxicated.[20]

Insanity

The most famous "capacity" defense is that of insanity. Actually, however, relatively few cases involve the insanity defense, since in many situations the person is so clearly mentally ill that the case never comes to trial. Nevertheless, the insanity defense raises important questions about the nature of capacity.

Most American courts follow the definition of insanity set forth in the English *M'Naghten* case of 1843. The **M'Naghten rule** defines insanity, for criminal law purposes, as a case in which the defendant "was labouring under such a defect of reason, from disease of the mind, as not to know the nature and quality of the act he was doing, or as not to know that what he was doing was wrong."[21]

This rule, when broken down, shows that the defendant must have a defect of reason caused by a disease of the mind, and that this defect either caused him or her not to know the nature and quality (or in modern terms, consequences) of his or her act, or caused him or her not to know that the act was wrong. A famous example of the first condition is that of a defendant who, while strangling his wife, believes that he is squeezing lemons instead. An example of the second condition would be a delusional assassin who kills a public official because he believes that God has ordered him to carry out the assassination in order to save the human race from destruction.

Some states have added the "irresistible impulse" test to the M'Naghten rule. Under this test, the defendant may understand the nature and consequences of his or her act, and that it is wrong, but he or she is unable to control his or her conduct, or in the words of one court, that he or she has "lost the power to choose between the right and wrong."[22]

While most states follow the M'Naghten rule, either with or without the irresistible impulse test, a number of states have adopted the rule set forth in the Model Penal Code, which is a somewhat easier test for a defendant to meet. This rule states that "a person is not responsible for criminal conduct if at the time of such conduct as a result of mental disease or defect he lacks the substantial capacity to appreciate the

criminality of his conduct or to conform his conduct to the requirements of the law." Unlike M'Naghten, it automatically includes an "irresistible impulse" kind of provision.[23]

Most insanity cases that do go to trial are death penalty cases. One
reason for this is that unlike other defenses, the insanity defense—if it
is successful—does not usually allow the defendant to go free. Instead,
a verdict of "not guilty by reason of insanity" normally means that the
defendant will be confined to a mental institution until he or she has
become sane. It is even possible that this open-ended commitment
might last longer than some prison terms for lesser crimes, which is
what makes the insanity defense unappealing to those who have committed such crimes. But in a mental institution, at least, the emphasis is
on treatment and not punishment.

A FINAL WORD ON MART RIDER

Although the Missouri Supreme Court reversed Mart Rider's conviction on the grounds that the trial judge should have told the jury to
consider the possibility that he had killed R. P. Tallent in self-defense,
Rider was tried again for Tallent's murder. In this second trial, the jury
did consider the self-defense argument but found Rider guilty anyway.
Rider was hanged in 1888.[24]

How was Rider able to appeal his case to another judge? Why did
he receive a new trial, and why did it not amount to double jeopardy?
These are questions about how the legal system investigates crimes and
tries criminals, an important part of the legal system known as criminal
procedure.

Criminal Procedure: Investigating the Crime

When Ernesto Miranda was arrested for robbery in Flagstaff, Arizona, in 1963, he had no way of knowing that his name would soon become one of the most famous in American criminal law. At that point he was merely one among thousands of suspects arrested that year, and the police treated him like any other. That treatment included an interrogation in the police station, without a lawyer present.

Two hours after the questioning started, Miranda signed a confession in which he admitted his guilt. Little is known of what happened during that interrogation to convince him to confess to a number of crimes. But it is known that police have sometimes used strong measures in interrogations—techniques sometimes called "the third degree"—including intimidation, lies, and threats of force. For most suspects, simply being in custody at a police station and under the scrutiny of uniformed officers can be unnerving.

In Miranda's case the confession, along with some other evidence, was enough for the jury to convict him. But what if the police had pushed too hard? What exactly had they said and done to Miranda during those two hours? Even if they had followed the law perfectly, what would happen if some dishonest or overzealous officer somewhere were to wring a false confession from an innocent person?

This was a danger that the U.S. Supreme Court wanted to deal with when it agreed to hear the case of *Miranda v. Arizona.* Noting that the Fifth Amendment to the federal Constitution forbade the government from forcing a person to incriminate him or herself, and that the Sixth Amendment gave the accused the right to the assistance of an attorney, the court declared that in the future law officers must make sure that all suspects knew of these rights before they were interrogated.

The result of this decision was the now famous "***Miranda*** warning" that is familiar to anyone who has watched an American crime drama on television. A famous version, usually heard on television when police arrest a suspect, is: "You have the right to remain silent. If you give up the right to remain silent, anything you say can and will be used against you in a court of law. You have the right to have an attorney present during questioning. If you cannot afford an attorney, one will be appointed for you." The suspect will then usually be asked if he or she understands these rights.[1]

Law officers must give the *Miranda* warning in most situations prior to questioning a suspect, regardless of the crime involved. The warning is an important part of the field of law known as criminal procedure—the law involving the investigation of crimes and the prosecution of suspected criminals.

Criminal procedure is a central part of the criminal law system in the United States at the local, state, and federal levels. In any criminal investigation and trial, the government with its great resources—everything from eavesdropping and other surveillance methods to crime laboratories to large numbers of detectives, other law officers, and trained prosecuting attorneys—is pitting itself against the individual, who typically has far fewer resources with which to defend him or herself. In other societies, moreover, the police have sometimes been used as an agency to oppress political, ethnic, or cultural groups as much as to enforce the law. Because of the potential dangers that criminal investigation poses to individual liberty, the rules of criminal procedure are in place to make sure that the government acts in a responsible fashion during criminal investigations and prosecutions. In the United States and other common law countries, these rules are an outgrowth of due process of law—the idea that government itself is bound to obey the law.

WARNING AS TO YOUR RIGHTS

You are under arrest. Before we ask you any questions, you must understand what your rights are.

You have the right to remain silent. You are not required to say anything to us at any time or to answer any questions. Anything you say can be used against you in court.

You have the right to talk to a lawyer for advice before we question you and to have him with you during questioning.

If you cannot afford a lawyer and want one, a lawyer will be provided for you.

If you want to answer questions now without a lawyer present you will still have the right to stop answering at any time. You also have the right to stop answering at any time until you talk to a lawyer.   P-4475

In the case of *Miranda v. Arizona*, the U.S. Supreme Court ruled that all law enforcement officers must read suspects their rights before questioning can begin. *MPI/Getty Images*

The notion of due process is as ancient as the earliest law codes, but the American tradition of due process began with **Magna Carta** ("Great Charter"), a famous English legal document of the thirteenth century. Prepared by some of England's leading nobles and signed by King John, Magna Carta was a set of limitations on the powers of the Crown. Chapter 39, in particular, states that "No Freeman shall be taken or imprisoned, or be [deprived of his land], or Liberties, or free Customs, or be outlawed, or exiled, or any other wise destroyed; nor will We not pass upon him, nor condemn him, but by lawful judgment of his Peers, or by the Law of the Land." In future documents, Parliament repeated this language, sometimes changing the phrase "law of the land" to "due process of law." This was the term used in some of the American colonies, and it was also the phrase used by the drafters of the Fifth and Fourteenth Amendments.

In addition to amending the Constitution with the original Fifth Amendment Due Process Clause, which is a general guarantee of government fairness, the authors of the Bill of Rights also listed several specific provisions in the Fourth, Fifth, Sixth, and Eighth Amendments

The concept of due process seen in the Fifth and Fourteenth Amendments has its roots in the Magna Carta, an English legal document drafted in 1215 A.D. *Press Association via AP Images*

dealing with criminal procedure. These provisions can be seen as out-growths of due process, reflecting the particular concerns and experiences of the former British colonists as well as their understanding of English history. Very broadly, these provisions fall into two categories:

1. Rights of suspects that the government must observe when it investigates criminal activity.
2. Rights that defendants, or accused persons, have during their trials.

This chapter will examine the first category, and the following chapter shall study the second.

THE FOURTH AMENDMENT: SEARCH, SEIZURE, ARREST, AND WARRANTS

The criminal justice process begins when a law enforcement agency or a prosecutor discovers that a crime has been committed. This can happen in different ways. A victim may report the crime, or perhaps a patrolling police officer notices some suspicious activity. An automated burglar alarm may summon police, or undercover agents might attempt to discover criminal activity by infiltrating a suspected drug ring or (as in the last chapter) encouraging a public official to accept a bribe. In all of these situations, the key element is that of investigation.

Most police resources are aimed at solving crimes that have already occurred and are known to them, although police also devote some time and energy to discovering unknown crimes and anticipating and preventing future crimes. In solving a known crime, police must do several things. These include discovering the identity of the perpetrator, collecting evidence of the perpetrator's guilt, and locating and arresting the perpetrator. To achieve these goals, police must gather information in various ways, a process collectively called investigation. This can range from looking through the window of the car a suspect is driving, to interviewing witnesses to a crime, to frisking a suspect for weapons, to collecting DNA or other physical evidence at a crime scene, to putting a suspect under surveillance. In all of these situations, and many more, the issue is how far officers may go in their investigation.[2]

Some people might instinctively think that law enforcement officials should be able to do anything necessary to bring criminals to justice. But a little thought will show how dangerous this can be to innocent persons. Suppose, for instance, that the police make an honest mistake in identifying a suspect or a street address, and as a result they kick in the door of a house late at night in order to arrest Dave and search his home. Because of their mistake, they have raided the wrong house; Cathy, who lives down the block, is the actual criminal. Perhaps Cathy has even deliberately "framed" Dave, making police think that Dave is the guilty one. Because of the officers' mistake, Dave has suffered a major, possibly traumatic, invasion of his privacy even though he is entirely innocent. His home may be ransacked and his belongings damaged; he may suffer serious physical injury in the raid, as well as humiliation at being led away in handcuffs as his neighbors look on. Even if the officers quickly realize their mistake, the damage may be hard or impossible to repair. Likewise, if police interrogate a suspect in the absence of an attorney, either the police or the suspect may make honest mistakes, either in speaking or in recalling or understanding what was said, that can lead prosecutors and juries to believe that the suspect is guilty even when he had nothing to do with the crime. Even with the safeguards of criminal procedure, this sort of episode has happened all too frequently. Without them, it would happen much more often.[3]

Another important point to remember is that in the American legal system, those accused of crimes are presumed to be innocent until they are proven (or plead) guilty. This **presumption of innocence** is an important safeguard against excessive government power because it forces the government to make out a convincing case (which it must prove beyond a reasonable doubt) that the defendant is guilty. The defendant, on the other hand, does not need to prove anything, although in nearly every case he or she will try to show the weaknesses and flaws in the government's case by introducing his or her own evidence.

These concerns for individuals' privacy, dignity, and security from government intrusion are crucial aspects of the American criminal justice system, and they are traceable back to colonists' unpleasant experiences during the American Revolution. The general search warrants known as the writs of assistance, which allowed officers to search any dwelling for any illegal goods at any hour of the day, were highly invasive of peoples' privacy without any concern for their innocence or guilt. The Fourth Amendment is a direct response to the sweeping powers of the writs of assistance.

The Fourth Amendment has two main provisions. The first commands that "The right of the people to be secure in their persons, houses, papers, and effects, against unreasonable searches and seizures, shall not be violated," while the second declares that "no Warrants shall issue, but upon probable cause, supported by Oath or affirmation, and particularly describing the place to be searched, and the persons or things to be seized." The general meaning of these passages is clear:

The government's power to investigate crime is limited by a concern for individual privacy and security from undue government interference. Nevertheless, many questions about the amendment's exact meaning have arisen over the years.

One of the main questions is about the relationship between the amendment's two provisions. If police carry out a search or seizure without a warrant, is that search or seizure *automatically* unreasonable? (To put this another way, does the second provision say what searches under the first provision are reasonable?) Or does the first provision allow searches and seizures to take place even without warrants, as long as they are reasonable? (To put this another way, is the first provision an exception to the second provision?)

While the Supreme Court has stated that warrants are generally necessary, over time it has carved out exceptions to this rule, allowing warrantless searches and seizures in an increasing number of situations, most often when taking time to obtain a warrant would be hard or impossible, creating a danger for the police or public.[4]

What Is a "Search"?

When a defendant wishes to argue that the government has violated his or her Fourth Amendment rights, the first step is to decide whether a "search," or perhaps a "seizure," has occurred at all. Originally the

WARRANTS

In criminal law, a warrant is an order, usually for search of premises, seizure of evidence of crime, or arrest of a suspected criminal, issued by a judge. In the American legal system, judges are not law enforcement officers; instead, in criminal cases, they are referees between the government and its citizens. The Fourth Amendment's warrant requirement, therefore, places law officers under the supervision of a neutral party in order to make sure that they follow the requirements of due process and other constitutional safeguards when carrying out criminal investigations.

Supreme Court understood search to mean some sort of physical invasion or examination of "houses, persons, papers, and effects." But as the
times and technology changed, the Court faced new problems that led
it to rethink this position. Since electronic eavesdropping usually does
not physically intrude onto a suspect's property, and thermal imaging
and metal detectors do not require officers to touch him or her, the use
of such devices would not amount to searches under the original test,
even though they might well violate his or her privacy.

In 1967, therefore, in the *Katz* decision, the Supreme Court devised
two new tests. One states that when a person intends to keep things or
information from public exposure, then an attempt to discover them is
a search. The other test states that persons are entitled to a "reasonable
expectation of privacy," and that a violation of this expectation is also
a search. Under these new tests, then, electronic eavesdropping does
amount to a search. So, too, might be an officer's visual inspection of
the inside of a car through a window when he or she has pulled over a
driver for speeding. The *Katz* tests even protect persons making calls
in public phone booths. The point to remember in all cases is that, as
one justice has noted, "The Fourth Amendment protects people, not
places."[5] In the decision whether a search has occurred, the location of
the intrusion is less important than the privacy of the person against
whom it takes place. And, if these rules seem too restrictive, remember
that police are always free to obtain a warrant, as long as they can meet
the **probable cause** requirement.

The Warrant: Probable Cause

The Fourth Amendment requires that all warrants must be based on
"probable cause," but because it does not define the meaning of this
phrase, the Supreme Court has had to fashion a definition in a string
of cases. Probable cause certainly falls far short of "proof beyond a
reasonable doubt." In fact, despite the term *probable*, it may not even
rise to the level of preponderance or "more likely than not." One writer
has said that probable cause is greater than mere suspicion and less
than certainty, but the Court has not given much more of a definition
beyond this. Instead, it has largely chosen to focus on the particular
situation, that is, the exact nature of the crime and the specific facts

that law officers rely upon when they request a warrant. But the Court has held that a probable cause exists when a reasonable person would believe the facts that serve as a basis for a warrant.[6]

The Warrant: Particularity

The requirement that a warrant must "particularly describ[e] the place to be searched, and the persons or things to be seized" is the passage that is most clearly a reaction to the writs of assistance. As with probable cause, the test of whether a warrant's description of the place to be searched meets the particularity requirement is that of reasonableness. Does a warrant describe the place in such a way that officers can locate it with reasonable effort? If so, the description is good enough.

A warrant's description of things to be seized, though, needs to be fairly specific. A warrant that simply authorized officers to seize "evidence of crime," for example, would fail the particularity test. But what about a warrant that described, "cocaine, marijuana, and a semi-automatic handgun together with ammunition for that handgun" plus "other evidence of crime"? Depending on how thoroughly the warrant describes the particular evidence the police believe they will find, and how often the judges in that community include broad language such as "other evidence of crime," such a warrant may or may not meet the particularity test.[7]

Execution of the Warrant

Although the text of the Fourth Amendment does not state how soon police must execute a warrant once a judge has signed it, or whether they may enter the premises by force, or without warning, or at night, the Supreme Court has found that the amendment includes some unwritten requirements that have their basis in the common law. Generally, the longer the delay between the issuance and the execution of the warrant, the greater the chance that the conditions on which the warrant is based may change. (Suspects, for instance, may move or destroy the evidence, or they themselves may move to a different residence.) Officers should thus execute the warrant as soon as possible after a judge has issued it. Many warrants, in fact, contain an expiration date, usually a matter of several days, after which they are no longer valid.

AO93(Rev.5/83)Search Warrant

UNITED STATES DISTRICT COURT
FOR THE DISTRICT OF COLUMBIA

In the Matter of the Search of

Residence at ▓▓▓▓▓▓
Frederick, Maryland,   **SEARCH WARRANT**
owned by Bruce Edwards Ivins,
DOB ▓▓▓, SSN ▓▓▓▓

CASE NUMBER: $O7-524 M-01$

TO: __Postal Inspector Thomas F. Dellafera__   and any Authorized Officer of the United States

Affidavit(s) having been made before me by __Postal Inspector Thomas F. Dellafera__ who has reason to believe
that ☐ on the person or ☒ on the premises known as (name, description and or location)

Single Family Residence at ▓▓▓▓▓▓Frederick, Maryland, and large white shed on rear of
property, owned by Bruce Edwards Ivins, DOB▓▓▓ SSN▓▓▓▓

in the District of Maryland there is now concealed a certain person or property, namely (describe the person or property)

trace quantities of Bacillus anthracis or simulants thereof, hairs, textile fibers, lab equipment or materials
used in preparation of select agents, papers, tape, pens, notes, books, manuals, receipts, financial records of
any type, correspondence, address books, maps, handwriting samples, photocopy samples, photographs,
computer files, cellular phones, phone bills, electronic pager devices, other digital devices, or other
documentary evidence.

I am satisfied that the affidavits(s) and any recorded testimony establish probable cause to believe that the person or
property so described is now concealed on the person or premises above-described and establish grounds for the
issuance of this warrant.

YOU ARE HEREBY COMMANDED to search on or before $\underline{November\ 9,\ 2007}$
                                                                          (Date)
(not to exceed 10 days) the person or place named above for the person or property specified, serving this warrant and
making the search ☐ (in the daytime - 6:00 A.M. to 10:00 P.M.) ☑ (at any time in the day or night as I find reasonable
cause has been established) and if the person or property be found there to seize same, leaving a copy of this warrant and
receipt for the person or property taken, and prepare a written inventory of the person or property seized and promptly
return this warrant to the undersigned U.S. Judge/U.S. Magistrate Judge, as required by law.

OCT 31 2007 @ 5:08 pM

Date and Time Issued in Washington, DC pursuant to
the domestic terrorism search warrant provisions
of Rule 41(b)(3)

DEBORAH A. ROBINSON
U.S. MAGISTRATE JUDGE
Name and Title of Judicial Officer

Signature of Judicial Officer

DEBORAH A. ROBINSON
U.S. MAGISTRATE JUDGE

United States District Court
For the District of Columbia
A TRUE COPY
NANCY MAYER WHITTINGTON, Clerk

By
Deputy Clerk

In order to conduct a legal search of a suspect or a suspect's
property, law enforcement officials must present a search warrant
to a judge for approval. *AP Photo/ Department of Justice*

The law also discourages "no-knock" entries onto premises, in
which police may kick in or batter down a door without announcing
themselves, as well as entries at night. (Even the writs of assistance

generally only allowed searches during daylight hours.) Sometimes the warrant will specify such an entry; in other cases the test is whether police have a reasonable suspicion that announcing themselves before entering would be dangerous or futile. On the one hand, no-knock, forced, or nighttime entries may be necessary when there is a high risk that the suspect may try to destroy the evidence or to escape if the police announce themselves. (Classic examples include suspects who flush drug caches down the toilet or who leap onto a fire escape.) On the other hand, no-knock entries may often result in the destruction of property, an unnecessary invasion of privacy, and the risk of a violent response from the suspect that could cause injury or death of officers, bystanders, or him or herself. For these reasons, the law looks down on "no-knock" and nighttime entries even though it does permit them in some situations.[8]

Exceptions to the Warrant Requirement

The Supreme Court has allowed warrantless searches in several situations, usually when the delay involved would mean a risk of danger to officers or the public, or the likely disappearance or destruction of the evidence of a crime. But even these warrantless searches and seizures usually require probable cause.

Suppose, for instance, that police lawfully arrest Judith, a known drug dealer. At the moment of arrest, Judith reaches quickly inside her coat pocket. The police may "frisk" Judith for their own protection to make sure that she is not about to draw a weapon. Likewise, if Judith reaches suddenly for a desk drawer the police may search it as well. This is known as the **search incident to lawful arrest**. But officers would not be justified in searching Judith's entire home or office on this basis, or anything farther away than arm's length. (Of course, if the police have a warrant that permits a search of the entire home or office, then the wider search would be legal.)

What if police do have a warrant to search Judith's entire home for illegal drugs, and while conducting the search they see several illegal assault rifles on a table? Although their warrant does not authorize a search for illegal weapons, officers may still seize the assault rifles because they are in **plain view**.

Another example is the **automobile exception**, which despite its name actually applies to most vehicles. Because they are movable and likely to disappear after a stop, police may search them for evidence of crime without a warrant, as long as they have probable cause to do so.

Yet another classic case that often involves automobiles arises when police suspect a driver of being intoxicated. Because the driver's blood alcohol level is **evanescent evidence**—that is, it will decrease if officers delay a blood or breath test—they may proceed with the test without obtaining a warrant. But here, too, officers must have probable cause in order to administer it.[9]

The Exclusionary Rule

What happens when a court decides that a police search, either with or without a warrant, went too far and violated a suspect's Fourth Amendment rights? Theoretically, the law can and often does allow several ways to deal with this problem. The officers or agency that conducted the illegal search might be held liable for money damages in a civil lawsuit; they might even be subject to criminal prosecution themselves, or may at least become subject to an internal investigation. But by far the most important and widespread way of dealing with illegal searches is a doctrine known as the **exclusionary rule**. This rule holds that prosecutors may not use illegally seized evidence to prove the defendant's guilt.[10]

For instance, if police search Lewis's home without a warrant and without probable cause and discover a container of illegal drugs, the court will exclude, or suppress, these drugs as evidence. This action, of course, will make prosecution of Lewis for drug possession or trafficking hard or even impossible, depending on what other (legal) evidence the officers have. On the one hand, blocking the prosecution of Lewis, who appears almost certain to be a criminal, appears unjust. On the other, this rule is the surest way of deterring police from making illegal searches to begin with.

Suppose that police illegally arrest Terry, without a warrant and without probable cause. Moments later, Terry blurts out a confession that just before his arrest he sold illegal drugs to Pat. Using Terry's statement as probable cause, police chase down and arrest Pat, search her, and discover the drugs.

Viewed in isolation, the arrest of Pat seems legal, since Terry's statement about Pat gave the police probable cause to arrest Pat. But because Terry's arrest was illegal to begin with, all of the evidence that police got because of that arrest—including Terry's confession and Pat's drugs—is subject to the exclusionary rule. This doctrine is known as the **fruit of the poisonous tree**. Simply put, if a search, seizure, or arrest is illegal, any evidence that results from it, even if it is legally obtained, will also be excluded, or suppressed. Again, the main purpose of this doctrine is to discourage law officers from acting illegally in the first place.[11]

THE FIFTH AMENDMENT: THE PRIVILEGE AGAINST SELF-INCRIMINATION

The Self-Incrimination Clause of the Fifth Amendment reads, "No person . . . shall be compelled in any criminal case to be a witness against himself." Popularly known as "taking the Fifth," this **privilege against self-incrimination** applies at every phase of the criminal process, especially when police attempt to get a suspect to confess to a crime.

The privilege obviously applies when police use physical force or torture to coerce a suspect to confess, but it applies in other situations as well. One of the key elements of the privilege is compulsion. Suppose that police merely threaten to use force against a suspect, or tell him that they will arrest his wife if he does not confess? Or, instead of threatening something bad, suppose officers hold out the promise of some sort of reward; for instance, they promise to protect a suspect, Stephen, from a hit man, Phillip, if Stephen signs a confession. Police might carry on an interrogation for two days without a break, and without offering a suspect sufficient food, water, or sleep. Suppose police approach a wounded suspect at the hospital and prevent doctors from treating him or her until he or she has confessed. The courts have held that all of these amount to compulsion in violation of the privilege against self-incrimination.[12]

On the other hand, police may often use a suspect's personal characteristics, such as his physical appearance, his voice, and his fingerprints, to identify him as the perpetrator of a crime. Since this does not amount to testimony by the suspect, the privilege against self-incrimination does not apply. A more physically invasive blood or DNA test, however, while not covered by the privilege, may still run afoul of due process concerns. In one case, when a suspect swallowed illegal drugs upon his arrest in order to prevent police from seizing them, the police took him to the hospital and forcibly had his stomach pumped to retrieve the drugs. The Supreme Court ruled that this was a severe and illegal violation of the suspect's due process and privacy rights.[13]

THE SIXTH AMENDMENT: RIGHT TO ASSISTANCE OF COUNSEL

The right of access to an attorney, like the privilege against self-incrimination, has a special place in criminal procedure. Because arrest, and even questioning, may be unfamiliar and intimidating to most people, and because few suspects have any legal training, the best safeguard of their rights is the presence of a lawyer.

In *Escobedo v. Illinois*, the Supreme Court held that, as with the privilege against self-incrimination, the right to counsel is not limited to the actual trial. Instead, it is available in the investigation stage when police begin to focus in on a particular suspect, even before he or she is charged with a crime. When officers question a suspect in the absence of an attorney, the Court also noted, it is a strong indicator that the confession may have been coerced.[14]

Suspects also generally have a right for their attorneys to be present during line-ups (at which victims and witnesses try to pick out the perpetrator of a crime from a group of people with similar appearances) and some other identification procedures, in order to make sure that officers conduct them fairly. As with the privilege against self-incrimination, however, the right to counsel does not extend to procedures such as fingerprinting or photographing. Nor do suspects' attorneys normally appear before the final investigative process, the grand jury.

THE GRAND JURY

A criminal case usually begins with an investigation by law enforcement, but a second way, the grand jury, is also available.

Originating with the grand inquests of medieval England, the grand jury is a panel of up to two dozen citizens who can summon and question witnesses and subpoena papers in order to determine if crimes have been committed. Convened, or **empanelled**, by a court, today's grand jury relies heavily on the local prosecuting attorney (often known as the district attorney), a public official who asks the court to empanel it and who decides whom and what the jury is to investigate. At the federal level, the Fifth Amendment requires that all felony prosecutions must be based on either a **presentment** or an indictment, both of which are accusations by a grand jury. While many states also use grand juries, the Supreme Court has ruled that the Fifth Amendment does not require them to do so. Grand juries operate in secret in order to avoid tipping off the targets of their investigations and leading them to interfere with witnesses or flee the jurisdiction. The secrecy also encourages those with knowledge of crimes to speak freely, as well as protecting the reputations of persons who are investigated but not charged with crimes.[15]

The grand jury cannot only compel the appearance of witnesses but can also grant them immunity from prosecution in exchange for their honest testimony. This removes the danger of self-incrimination and encourages witnesses to speak freely even about crimes they may have committed, in order to discover incriminating information about other individuals. If a summoned witness fails to appear or a custodian of papers refuses to supply them on demand, the grand jury can find them in **contempt** and force them to pay fines or even serve jail time.

Because of its secrecy and its legal powers, the grand jury is especially useful in certain types of investigations. These include public corruption cases that law enforcement agencies and even prosecutors might be reluctant to pursue, as well as cases in which victims and witnesses are reluctant or afraid to cooperate with law enforcement, as they may be when the investigation involves large criminal organizations.

Grand jury witnesses have some, but not all, of the protections already discussed in this chapter. Grand juries do not need to meet the probable cause requirement when summoning witnesses or subpoenaing items, since a grand jury proceeding does not carry the stigma of an arrest, and because historically all citizens have always had a duty to appear before grand juries when summoned. If the grand jury required something more invasive than an appearance, however, such as blood or DNA testing, probable cause would likely be needed.[16]

The privilege against self-incrimination, however, does apply. Witnesses may not use the privilege to avoid testifying altogether, and prosecutors will not normally advise them of their right not to make incriminating statements, but they may nevertheless refuse to answer questions on those grounds. A grant of immunity, however, means that witnesses must answer the questions, since their answers cannot be used to prosecute them.

The right to counsel is generally not available in grand jury investigations, mainly because witnesses—even those who may be targets of the investigation—are not yet accused of a crime. The presence of defense lawyers in the grand jury hearings might interfere with witnesses' testimony.

Investigation is an important part of criminal procedure. The other main branch of criminal procedure is the process for dealing with individuals who are formally accused of crimes as a result of criminal investigations.

Criminal Procedure: The Trial

Duke Kahanamoku is famous for being the founder of the modern sport of surfing. Born in Hawaii in 1890, Kahanamoku grew up on Waikiki Beach, where he became an expert swimmer and surfer. Having broken world swimming records in amateur swim meets, Kahanamoku went on to compete in the Olympic Games of 1912, 1920, and 1924, winning a total of three gold and two silver medals in swimming. In 1925, using his surfboard, he rescued eight men from drowning when their fishing boat capsized. But in the legal world, Kahanamoku is best known for being a party in a famous Supreme Court case that arose during World War II.

Following the Japanese surprise attack on the American naval base at Pearl Harbor, Hawaii, on December 7, 1941, the Hawaiian government placed the territory (Hawaii was not yet a state) under martial law. This meant, among other things, that the U.S. military would try all crimes, and the civilian courts were prohibited from doing so. In the days after the Pearl Harbor attack, the danger of a Japanese invasion of the islands seemed very real. Only by placing the military in charge of Hawaii's security could the government safeguard against this danger.

In early 1944, Duke Kahanamoku was serving as the sheriff of Honolulu when Lloyd C. Duncan, a civilian shipyard worker at Pearl

Harbor, got into a brawl with two marine sentries at the navy yard. Because Hawaii was under martial law, the U.S. Army was in charge of all law enforcement in the territory. As a result, a military court, hearing the case without a jury, sentenced Duncan to six months in jail. By 1944 most of the danger to Hawaii had passed, and the civilian courts had reopened. Duncan thus asked the federal district court in Hawaii to intervene in his case, claiming that his trial by a military court was unconstitutional, violating his Fifth and Sixth Amendment rights to a fair trial. The court responded by ordering Sheriff Kahanamoku, who was holding Duncan in jail, to show his legal authority for doing so. Kahanamoku replied that martial law required him to hold Duncan prisoner.

The case of *Duncan v. Kahanamoku* went all the way to the Supreme Court. In 1946, a few months after World War II ended, the Court agreed that Duncan had been denied his constitutional rights to a fair trial. Because courts-martial need not follow all of the trial requirements of the Bill of Rights, the Court held, they could easily endanger those rights. "Courts and their procedural safeguards are indispensable to our system of government," Justice Hugo Black wrote for the majority. "They were set up by our founders to protect the liberties they valued."[1]

The *Duncan* decision explains why a criminal defendant has important rights in a criminal trial that may take his or her property, his or her liberty, or even his or her life, but it does not discuss exactly what those rights are. This chapter will examine them more closely.

The Anglo-American judicial process is an **adversarial system**. In this system, trials take place between two parties: the prosecution (or in a civil case the plaintiff) and the defense, or defendant. The prosecution is managed by a government lawyer known as the prosecutor, who represents the public. (For this reason, case names usually refer to the prosecution as "the People," "the State," or in federal criminal trials "the United States.") The defendant is the accused perpetrator of the crime.

In an adversarial system, moreover, it is up to the two parties to investigate the facts of the case and to present evidence to support their respective arguments. The prosecutor will try to prove that the defendant has committed a crime, while the defendant, through his or her attorney, will try to rebut, or show to be false, the prosecutor's evidence, or to produce evidence to show the defendant's innocence. While the judge, like the prosecutor, is a government employee, in an adversarial system he or she is not on the prosecutor's side. Instead, he or she is a neutral party who decides whether the actions, arguments, and evidence of both sides are legally acceptable. Unlike the prosecutor, the judge's job is not to convict the defendant but to ensure that both parties "play by the rules" in presenting their cases to the trial jury. Even in cases that do not involve a jury, in which the judge will determine the defendant's guilt or innocence, he or she still functions not as a prosecutor but as a neutral party.[2]

The adversarial system shapes the entire criminal process from the moment a suspect is arrested until the time he or she goes free or is found guilty and given a sentence. But only part of this process involves the courtroom trial. The criminal case must go through several stages before the actual trial begins, and it often moves through several stages afterward. The stages are usually grouped into the post-arrest or pretrial phase, the trial itself, and the post-trial phase. The exact procedures and steps vary from state to state, and even within a state depending on the gravity of the crime; the following discussion is a general view of the process.

THE PRE-TRIAL PHASE

After an arrest, the first step of a criminal case involves "booking" the suspect, or preparing a record of his or her arrest and identity. As part of this process, the police photograph and fingerprint a suspect. For some minor offenses, the police at this stage may also release the suspect on **station-house bail**: If the suspect pays a sum of money and promises to appear in court at a set date and time, he or she will be released from custody. If he or she then fails to appear in court as required, he or she forfeits the money. But if the suspect is under arrest for a felony or a serious misdemeanor, he or she will remain in custody until he or she appears before a **magistrate**, a minor judge who has the authority to issue warrants, review arrests, set bail, and carry out some other judicial functions. Normally this **first appearance** must take place within about 48 hours, depending on the rules of the jurisdiction.

Between the suspect's booking and his or her first appearance, the police may continue to investigate the crime and collect evidence. During this time the police as well as the prosecutor also review the evidence in order to decide whether the arresting officer or officers properly charged the suspect. The police supervisors who carry out this review may approve the original charge, or they may raise it to a more serious charge. They may also reduce it to a less serious level, or they may even decide not to pursue charges at all (in which case the suspect will be released immediately). The prosecutor carries out the same sort of review independently of the police, also choosing among these same options.

Police review of the charges is important because if the police decide to release the suspect, the prosecutor will probably not even become involved and the case is over. On the other hand, even if the police approve the charge, the case cannot move forward unless the prosecutor agrees. In that case the police must release the suspect even if they continue to believe that he has committed the crime.[3]

This raises the sort of question that came up in the *Kahanamoku* case. What if the police simply decided to hold a suspect in jail without ever charging him or her or bringing him or her before a magistrate or other judge? If this were to happen, the suspect could seek a court order known as a writ of habeas corpus, literally meaning, "You have the body." Habeas corpus is a court order to someone holding a person in custody (usually a law officer) ordering the officer to show why that person is being held. If the police cannot then show a legal reason for the detention, the court will order the prisoner's release. Habeas corpus is the type of court order that Lloyd Duncan got against Duke Kahanamoku in 1944. It is an important tool that stops the government from holding people prisoner without trial and for no reason. It is so important a safeguard against government abuse of power, in fact, that it is the only writ specifically mentioned in the federal Constitution, which requires habeas corpus to be available at all times with only a few very rare exceptions.[4]

If both the police and the prosecutor approve the charges, the prosecutor will then file a **criminal complaint** with the magistrate. At this point the suspect officially becomes a defendant in a criminal legal action. At his or her first appearance, the magistrate will notify the defendant of the charges against him or her. The magistrate will also advise him or her of his or her right to remain silent and his or her right to a lawyer, and will appoint an attorney if the defendant requests it. Another important step during the first appearance is for the magistrate to verify that there is probable cause for moving forward with the case.

Finally, the magistrate will set **bail**. As with station-house bail, this involves the defendant's payment of money, or at least a promise to pay, in exchange for his or her release from custody until his or her next court appearance. The magistrate may release the defendant on his or her own recognizance if he or she is known in the community, although he or she may confiscate the defendant's passport to ensure that he or she does not leave the country. For serious crimes, the magistrate may require a large amount of bail, or deny bail altogether, requiring the defendant to stay in custody until the trial.

The Eighth Amendment to the federal Constitution prohibits courts from imposing "excessive bail." But this does not mean that all defendants have a right to be released on bail; courts may deny bail in many situations. Instead, "excessive" simply means that the court should look at both the gravity of the crime and the defendant's ability to pay. If the magistrate decides to require bail, then in light of the particular crime it should be large enough to motivate the defendant to show up for the trial. Anything more than this would likely be excessive.[5]

After the first appearance, the proceedings can move in different directions depending on the jurisdiction as well as on the particular case. Most states require a **preliminary hearing**, which takes place a few weeks after the first appearance. In this proceeding the defendant's lawyer is present along with the prosecutor. Here, again, the magistrate will make sure that the prosecutor has probable cause to believe that the defendant committed the crime, and he or she may require the prosecutor to present witnesses to support his or her probable cause claim. The defendant's lawyer will also examine the prosecutor's witnesses. If the magistrate finds that probable cause exists, he or she will **bind the case over** either to a grand jury or directly to a trial court.[6]

Depending on the jurisdiction, however, either the prosecutor or the defendant may choose to bypass the preliminary hearing altogether.

If the defendant wants to move on to the trial, or he or she intends to plead guilty, he or she may waive the preliminary hearing. In states and cases in which a grand jury indictment or presentment is required, the prosecutor, too, may skip the preliminary hearing, since the fact of the indictment itself will show that probable cause exists.

After the preliminary hearing in states that do not require an indictment, the prosecutor will file an **information**, or accusation, with the trial court. The information is an official charge, based on the police and prosecutor's investigation and supported by probable cause, that the defendant committed a specified crime or crimes. An information, an indictment, or a presentment is needed to move forward with the case at this point, again depending on the jurisdiction.[7]

At this point the defendant often has one more pretrial court appearance, which is called the **arraignment**. This is an appearance before the trial court itself, at which time the judge will ask the defendant how he or she pleads. (When the charge is a minor one, this step may take place at one of the earlier appearances.) If the defendant pleads not guilty, or not guilty by reason of insanity, the case then moves on to trial. This is called "joining the issue," which means that one party to a case asserts a fact (in this case, the defendant's guilt) to be true, and the other denies it. The purpose of the trial is to decide the issue.

At each of the above stages, from arrest down to the arraignment, the decision maker (the police, the prosecutor, the magistrate, the grand jury, or the judge) faces a basic choice whether to move the case forward because he or she has reason to believe that the defendant committed a crime, or instead to end the proceedings and release the defendant. At every stage, significant numbers of suspects are released either for lack of probable cause or because the police or prosecutor decide that prosecution is not appropriate for some reason. In fact, well under a third of felony cases go all the way to trial.[8]

A major factor that reduces the number of trials is the practice of **plea bargaining**. This is an agreement in which the defendant agrees to plead guilty in exchange for some action on the part of the prosecutor.

There are several types of plea agreement. In one type, the defendant pleads guilty to a less serious crime than the prosecutor has charged him or her with. This usually guarantees the defendant a lesser sentence while at the same time guaranteeing the prosecutor a conviction. Or the defendant may agree to plead guilty to the crime with which he or she is charged in exchange for a promise from the prosecutor to seek a reduced sentence. A third type of plea agreement is for a defendant who is accused of multiple crimes to plead guilty to one of them in exchange for the prosecutor's dropping of the other charges.

Plea bargaining achieves several goals. In the first place, it provides a certain and successful end to the prosecution. While most criminal cases that go to trial end with a conviction (largely because the many pretrial phases have already eliminated the most questionable cases), the trial is still always something of a gamble for both parties, since no one knows for sure what the jury will decide or what sentence the judge will choose to impose on a guilty defendant. The plea agreement allows the parties to avoid this gamble; the prosecutor gets a conviction, while the defendant gets a more lenient sentence than he might otherwise risk getting. A plea agreement also lets both parties avoid the time, stress, and expense of a trial, all of which may be considerable (especially in major felony cases). If the law of a state sets up a rigid sentencing system, prosecutors may also find that a plea agreement allows a more just sentence than a trial could produce.[9]

THE TRIAL

Those cases that have not been resolved after the arraignment ultimately go on to trial. The first step in this phase is the selection of a petit jury, or trial jury, which usually consists of 12 members. Some states may use a smaller number, such as six, and while the Sixth Amendment ensures the defendant's right to a jury trial, he or she may waive that right. When this occurs, known as **bench trials**, the judge will decide the defendant's innocence or guilt.

The process of jury selection, known as *voir dire*, is designed to produce a panel of impartial jurors who can decide the case fairly. During voir dire, the prosecutor and the defense attorney question each potential juror. If either attorney believes that a juror's answers show him or her to be biased, he or she may **challenge** the juror, at which point the judge will typically dismiss him or her from service.

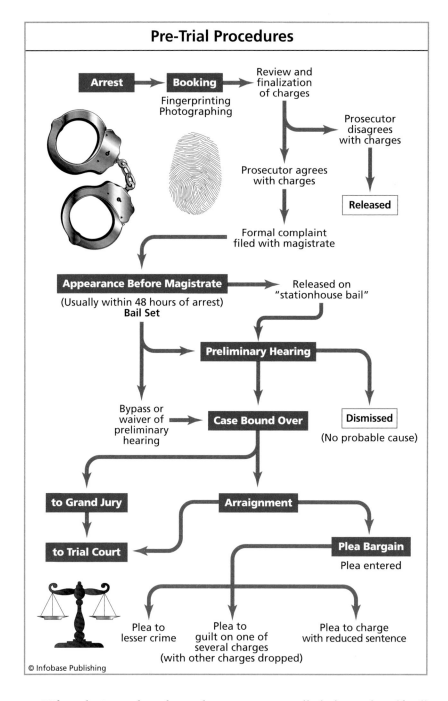

Pre-Trial Procedures

Arrest → **Booking** → Review and finalization of charges

Fingerprinting
Photographing

Prosecutor disagrees with charges

Prosecutor agrees with charges

Released

Formal complaint filed with magistrate

Appearance Before Magistrate → Released on "stationhouse bail"

(Usually within 48 hours of arrest)
Bail Set

Preliminary Hearing

Bypass or waiver of preliminary hearing → **Case Bound Over**

Dismissed
(No probable cause)

to Grand Jury

Arraignment

to Trial Court

Plea Bargain
Plea entered

Plea to lesser crime

Plea to guilt on one of several charges (with other charges dropped)

Plea to charge with reduced sentence

© Infobase Publishing

When the jurors have been chosen, or empanelled, the trial itself will begin. The first stage in the actual trial is that of the opening statements. The prosecutor will begin by describing the case as well as the elements of the crime involved, and summarizing what he or she will try to prove with the evidence he will present. This will help jurors understand the significance of the evidence when the prosecutor presents it later. After the prosecutor finishes, the defense attorney may make his own opening statement, although in some jurisdictions he or she will not do so until the prosecutor has finished presenting his or her evidence.[10]

The next stage is the presentation of the prosecution's case. In order to win a conviction, the prosecutor has the burden of proving beyond a reasonable doubt all of the elements of the crime of which the defendant stands accused. Failure to prove even one of the elements will mean an **acquittal**, or a finding of not guilty. For instance, if the defendant is charged with the crime of knowingly possessing stolen property, the prosecutor must prove beyond a reasonable doubt both that the defendant was in possession of stolen property and that he or she knew that it was stolen. To prove these elements, the prosecutor will rely on two main types of evidence: **real evidence** and **witness** testimony.

Real evidence is anything tangible, such as a surveillance camera photograph or tape that shows a defendant holding up a bank or a convenience store, or the actual crowbar that a defendant used to force open a door or window. In the "knowing possession of stolen property" case it might even be the property itself, perhaps jewelry or weapons.

In witness testimony the prosecutor will summon a witness who then swears or affirms that he or she will give a truthful account of his or her experience. The prosecutor will then ask the witness a series of questions designed to help the witness provide information that helps prove his or her case. In a reckless driving case, for instance, the witness may testify that the defendant drove past her at a high rate of speed. This questioning is known as **direct examination**.

Immediately after a prosecutor has finished direct examination, the defendant's attorney will often **cross-examine** the same witness. Cross-examination is a series of questions designed to show that there is "another side" to the witness's experience that is more favorable to the defendant. During cross-examination, the reckless driving witness may admit that the defendant was driving his severely injured son to the hospital, a fact that she did not mention during direct examination. Cross-examination might also have the goal of showing that the witness herself lacks **credibility**, or believability. To challenge the witness's

A prosecutor cross-examines a psychiatrist during a murder trial. *AP Photo/Herb Nygren Jr., File*

credibility, the defense attorney might ask her how close she was to the defendant's car as it passed her; if she answers that she was in a field a half-mile away, then a doubt arises as to whether she could have been sure that the defendant was the one who was driving it. (Note that in this case the witness might not be lying about the driver's identity; she might merely be honestly mistaken.)

After cross-examination, the prosecutor may examine the witness again (the **re-direct examination**) to address any weaknesses in her testimony that the cross-examination may have revealed. In this case, the prosecutor may ask if the witness has ever known anyone but the defendant to drive that particular car. She might reply by noting that because it was a valuable car to which he was very attached, he never permitted even other family members to drive it. This strengthens the credibility of her identification of the driver even if she saw the car from a distance. Following this is the **re-cross examination** in which the defendant once again seeks to show weaknesses in the witness's testimony.

One witness that the prosecutor may not summon in a criminal case is the defendant him or herself. This is one of the major differences between a criminal trial and a civil trial. The Fifth Amendment privilege against self-incrimination prevents a prosecutor from questioning the criminal defendant at all unless the defendant him or herself decides to be a witness.

When the prosecutor has finished presenting his or her evidence, the defense attorney may make an opening statement if he or she did not do so at the trial's beginning. Then he or she presents his or her own evidence in the same way as the prosecutor. Witness testimony will follow the same pattern of direct and cross-examination that it did before, except that now the defense attorney is the one who summons witnesses and conducts the direct examinations, with the prosecutor cross-examining them.

Technically, the defendant does not need to prove his or her innocence, and so theoretically he or she and his or her attorney are not required to present any evidence at all. The burden is on the prosecutor to prove the defendant's guilt. In fact, if the prosecutor has obviously not met this burden (for instance, perhaps he or she has failed to present any evidence establishing the existence of one of the elements of the crime), then the defendant may simply ask the court to dismiss the case.

But if the prosecutor has introduced credible evidence to suggest that the defendant is guilty, the defense will then probably introduce its own evidence to challenge the prosecutor's version of events. For instance, in the reckless driving case, the defense may call a witness who testifies that three other people in the defendant's town own cars that are identical to the defendant's. This testimony will reduce the impact of the prosecution witness's identification of the defendant based solely on her (possibly erroneous) recognition of his car. (Of course, this witness will then be subject to the prosecutor's cross-examination, followed, perhaps, by re-direct and re-cross). The defense may also introduce evidence designed to establish the existence of a justification or excuse of the sort studied earlier. In this case, the defendant might introduce evidence to show that the necessity defense applies, since the fact of the life-threatening injury to the defendant's son placed him under a duty to get him medical help as quickly as possible.[11]

Throughout the trial, the prosecutor and defense must abide by a considerable number of rules and constitutional requirements. Each state, for instance, provides a set of **rules of evidence** that control not only what kind of evidence a party may present but also even how he or she presents it. For instance, each attorney may generally ask only questions (and witnesses may only give answers) that are **relevant** to the proof or disproof of the matters before the court. Another example is the **hearsay rule**. Under this rule, if Tony, a witness, testifies that Ceres, who is not a witness, told him that Jeffrey was driving the car, Tony's statement is not evidence that Ceres believed Jeffrey was the driver. In general, the concept of hearsay is "Tony said that Ceres said." Since Ceres is not in court and the opposing party cannot cross-examine her, Tony's statement about what Ceres said is inadmissible. (The hearsay rule, however, is famous for its many exceptions, which rules of evidence also list.)

There are many other rules besides relevance and hearsay, ranging from the qualifications of **expert witnesses** who have some specialized knowledge that might help the jury understand the facts of the case better to the requirements for admitting documents and other real evidence.[12] The rules may even control the exact way in which an attorney may ask a witness a question. In some circumstances, an attorney may ask a witness a question in such a way that it suggests a certain answer (a **leading question**). In the reckless driving case, a leading question might be "When you looked at the road, you saw what appeared to be the defendant's car rushing by, correct?" A nonleading question, on the other hand, might be "When you looked at the road, what did you see?" The rules of evidence control exactly when an attorney may lead a witness in this fashion.

In addition to the rules of evidence, the defendant has a number of constitutional rights besides the ones already discussed. Most of these rights appear in the Sixth Amendment to the federal Constitution, although other rights may appear in state constitutions as well.

One important right found in the Sixth amendment is the right to a **speedy trial**. Once criminal proceedings have begun, they create a stigma against the defendant, so the delay of a trial for longer than a reasonable time is unfair to him or her. Today, on average, the time from the arrest of a defendant for most major crimes to his or her trial date is somewhat less than a year. A delay of significantly more than a year would raise the speedy trial issue.[13]

Another important Sixth Amendment requirement is that all criminal trials be **public**. This helps ensure that trial courts will conduct themselves fairly because of public scrutiny. Yet another right is that of **compulsory process**, which gives the defendant the ability to subpoena witnesses, papers, and other evidence, which the prosecutor may also do. The defendant also has the right to **confront** the witnesses against him or her; this is to prevent prosecutors from making up a charge against a defendant and then stopping him or her from answering those charges effectively. (The defendant's cross-examination of prosecution witnesses is a major aspect of this right.)[14]

In a jury trial, the judge and jury have very different jobs. A well-known saying is that the jury finds the facts while the judge finds the law. What this means, in effect, is that both the prosecution and the defense are trying to tell their stories to the jury—to explain what they each believe happened. The prosecutor will set forth one version of events (in which the defendant is guilty) and the defendant will set forth another version (in which he or she is innocent). The jury's role is to decide which of these stories is more accurate, or to put this another way, to decide what actually happened.[15]

The judge's role, on the other hand, is to make sure that both parties play by the rules of evidence and other laws. In other words, he or she uses the law to control the flow of information from the parties to the jury. A famous example of how this works is when one attorney asks a witness a question that the other attorney believes violates the rule of relevance, the hearsay prohibition, or some other rule. The opposing attorney will object; the judge must then decide whether the rule permits the question, in which case he or she will overrule the objection, or whether instead the rule does forbid the question, in which case he or she will sustain the objection.[16]

Once the defense lawyer has finished presenting his or her evidence, the prosecutor may introduce still more evidence during the **rebuttal** stage. This is similar to a re-direct examination in that the prosecutor is introducing new evidence designed to show the weaknesses in all of the evidence that the defendant has presented. There may even be a **rejoinder** stage, in which the defendant introduces evidence to answer the evidence the prosecutor has presented in his rebuttal. At last, however, both parties rest their cases, completing their presentation of evidence.[17]

Each attorney then presents a **closing argument**, or **summation**. Resembling the opening statement, a closing argument sums up and explains the evidence that a party has presented. Although an attorney may not introduce new evidence during his or her closing argument, he or she may give an overview of the evidence he or she has already presented in order to convince the jury to accept his or her view of the case. Typically, the defense attorney presents his or her closing argument before the prosecutor, who gets the "last word" since he or she has the burden of proving the defendant's guilt.[18]

Following the closing arguments, the judge **charges**, or instructs, the jury. These instructions will usually deal with three major subjects. First, the judge will explain the legal definition of the crime or crimes of which the defendant is accused, together with each legal defense that the evidence suggests might apply. Second, the judge will also explain legal principles of evidence and proof, telling the jury what evidence it must consider as well as what it must not consider. The judge will also remind the jury of the presumption of the defendant's innocence and the prosecutor's burden of proof beyond a reasonable doubt. Finally, the judge will explain how the jury is to reach its decision, covering such matters as discussion and voting.[19]

The **jury charge** highlights the different roles of the judge and the jury. Usually judges may not tell the jury what evidence it must believe or must not believe, or how believable they themselves found the evidence. Instead, the judge in effect merely tells the jury that *if* it believes, based on the evidence, that all of the elements of the crime are present, then—and only then—it may find the defendant guilty of the crime. (The judge will follow the same pattern as to any defenses that the defendant has raised.) In some cases, however, such as when the judge finds that the evidence, even if viewed in the light most favorable to the prosecution, fails to show that all elements of the crime existed, he or she may dismiss the case without even letting the jury vote.[20]

The actual jury deliberations are closed and confidential. Traditionally, a vote to convict or acquit had to be unanimous, but the Supreme Court has held that a 12-member state jury may convict a defendant by

A defendant and her lawyer stand before the judge awaiting the verdict in a custodial interference case. *AP Photo/Kitsap Sun, Carolyn J. Yaschur*

a vote of 11-1 or even 10-2. If a state uses a six-person jury, however, the vote must still be unanimous.[21] If a jury is unable to agree after a reasonable time as to the defendant's guilt or innocence, the judge will declare a mistrial.

If the jury does reach an agreement, however, it announces its **verdict** ("true declaration"), finding the defendant guilty, not guilty, or not guilty by reason of insanity on each separate charge. If the defendant has been found not guilty, or acquitted, of all charges, the trial ends and he goes free immediately. If he is found guilty, or **convicted**, of one or more crimes, then he faces sentencing. The case then moves into the post-trial phase.

THE POST-TRIAL PHASE

The sentencing process, especially for more serious crimes, varies widely from state to state. On the one hand, the Constitution's Eighth Amendment prohibits courts from imposing "cruel and unusual punishments," and state legislatures, along with Congress, have put limits on the maximum and minimum sentences that courts may hand down for particular crimes. On the other hand, because the facts of every case and the circumstances of every defendant differ, courts need some flexibility in sentencing in order to achieve the goals of the criminal law (including incapacitation, deterrence, reform, and retribution). In jury trials, both the judge and jury may have a role in sentencing, especially in **capital** cases (those which may involve the death penalty). Depending on the state, as well as the particular offense, the jury may have no role in sentencing, or it may recommend a sentence to the judge, or it may have the entire responsibility of deciding the sentence. In capital cases, many states have a separate hearing for determining the sentence, during which the prosecution and the defense call witnesses and submit evidence as they did during the trial itself. Penalties may range from **probation**—a period of time during which the convicted defendant, while free, is subject to judicial supervision and may be required to meet certain conditions in order to avoid more serious punishment—to payment of a fine, to prison time of months or years, to execution.

Appeals

A convicted defendant may appeal his or her case to a higher, or **appellate**, court, if he or she believes that some legal error (or errors) have occurred during his or her case. He or she may argue, for instance, that the magistrate in his or her case mistakenly decided that probable cause existed or that the trial judge wrongly allowed the jury to hear some evidence that should have been excluded (perhaps because it was prejudicial or hearsay). An **appeal** is not a retrial of the facts of the case; instead it focuses on whether the magistrates and trial judge correctly interpreted the legal rules during the trial.

States generally have two levels of appellate court, often (but not always) called the court of appeals and the supreme court. At the federal level, the highest court is the United States Supreme Court, and a second level of regional appellate courts are known as the federal Courts of Appeals.

If an appellate court does find that significant legal errors occurred in the defendant's case, it may **reverse** his or her conviction outright, in which case he or she goes free, or it may **remand** the case for a new trial. It may **vacate** the sentence while upholding the conviction, in which case the trial court will need to resentence the defendant. On the other hand, it may **affirm** the decision of the trial court, in which case the verdict and the sentence continue to stand. In this case, the defendant may appeal to the highest appellate court, which can also reach any of these same outcomes. If the defendant in a state case believes that the proceedings against him or her have violated his or her federal rights, he or she may even, in some circumstances, take his or her case before a federal appellate court.

Double Jeopardy

The possibility of a new trial raises another important issue. The Fifth Amendment provides that no one shall "be subject for the same offense to be twice put in jeopardy of life or limb." This means that once the criminal law process has placed a person in jeopardy of life or limb (and by extension liberty), then it may not do so a second time for the same crime. Generally, jeopardy "attaches," or occurs, once a trial jury has been empanelled and sworn, but there are exceptions. While a jury's acquittal of a defendant means that he or she absolutely may not be tried again in that jurisdiction for that crime, what if a mistrial takes place before the jury reaches a verdict? What if the trial judge dismisses the case because the prosecution has engaged in misconduct? Suppose an appellate court has remanded a case because of a trial judge's legal error? All of these situations raise the basic problem of double jeopardy: the importance of the defendant's security from an embarrassing, expensive, ongoing or repeated harassment by the state on the one hand and society's interest in bringing criminals to justice on the other.

Given this balance, then, if a dismissal takes place before the jury reaches a verdict for reasons other than a lack of evidence, or the judge declares a mistrial, and the defendant agrees to these decisions, a new trial may take place. A new trial may also occur if an appeals court has found a legal error in the original trial, given the fact that it is the defendant who has appealed the case and asked for a review of that trial.

If a state has two crimes on its books that have the same elements, and the defendant is tried and acquitted of one of them, then the Double Jeopardy Clause prohibits the state from trying him or her for the other offense. On the other hand, if the state and federal governments both have statutes making the defendant's conduct criminal and he or she is tried and acquitted in either state or federal court, the other court system may still try him or her for the other offense without violating double jeopardy.[22]

Habeas Corpus

A state defendant who has been convicted of a crime and who has exhausted all of his or her appeals in the state courts has one final option. When a convicted defendant believes that the state proceedings violated his or her rights under the federal Constitution, he or she may seek a writ of habeas corpus from a federal court. Habeas corpus is a court order requiring an officer who holds someone prisoner to show the legal basis for doing so. When a state prisoner seeks a federal writ of habeas corpus, he or she is asking the federal court to have the state government show that it has abided by the federal Constitution in its proceedings against the defendant. If the federal courts find that the state proceedings violated the defendant's constitutional rights, the federal court may go so far as to order the state to release the defendant from prison.

On the one hand, federal habeas corpus review of state criminal proceedings helps to ensure that state courts observe defendants' federal constitutional rights. On the other hand, this process has resulted in thousands of habeas corpus requests each year (most of them finding that the state proceedings were carried out properly), which can clog the operations of the federal courts.[23]

The criminal trial process can be a long and complex one, especially when serious crimes are involved. The legal system faces a special situation when the perpetrator of a crime is a child.

The Juvenile
Court System

Little is known about Mary Ann Crouse. Born in the early 1800s, she was living in Philadelphia, and probably around the age of 10 or 15, when she first began causing her parents some difficulty. We do not even know exactly what that difficulty was, except that her mother called her behavior "vicious," and it was serious enough for others to notice it. Whatever Mary Ann was doing, it made her impossible for her mother to control. Perhaps it involved gambling, or maybe her conduct was so destructive—or self-destructive—that her mother decided that Mary Ann would never be able to attract a husband. At any rate, her mother feared that Mary Ann would become a pauper, unable to support herself or find anyone who would provide for her. To put it simply, Mary Ann Crouse was trouble.

Finally, around late 1838, the girl's mother went before a magistrate with an extreme request. Thirteen years earlier, Pennsylvania had established a "house of refuge," something like a reform school for housing children who had committed crimes, or whose parents either could not or would not care for them properly because of their—or maybe even the parents'—behavior. While the house of refuge was no jail, it was no vacation spot, either. Mary Ann's mother apparently believed that the girl belonged there, so she asked the magistrate to commit her to the house of refuge. Based on the witnesses that came forward who agreed about Mary Ann's behavior, the magistrate ordered the commitment.

But if Mary Ann's mother had given up hope, her father had not. In fact, he disagreed so strongly with Mary Ann's commitment that he sought a writ of habeas corpus demanding that the managers of the house of refuge show their legal authority for holding Mary Ann. Representing him was William L. Hirst, one of Philadelphia's star attorneys. Hirst's argument was a simple one: No matter how badly children behaved, the state did not have the power to take them away from their parents.

The Supreme Court of Pennsylvania disagreed, siding instead with the house of refuge and its attorney Jared R. Ingersoll, another famous lawyer of the day. The court's ruling was short and direct. "The public has a paramount interest in the virtue and knowledge of its members, and … of strict right, the business of education belongs to it," it declared. If parents could not or would not raise and educate a child properly, then the state had both the right and the duty to raise and teach the child, for the good of both the child and the community.

This welfare of the child was very important to the court, which pointed out that the house of refuge, while strict, was not the same as a prison designed for children's punishment. Its goal was "reformation, by training its inmates to industry; by imbuing their minds with principles of morality and religion; by furnishing them with means to earn a living; and, above all, by separating them from the corrupting influence of improper associates." For these reasons, the court ruled, Mary Ann's confinement in the house of refuge was legal.

Mary Ann's was one of the first cases to discuss the power of the government to oversee the interests of an at-risk child. As such, it is one of the foundations of the modern juvenile justice system.[1]

In some ways, the juvenile court system is very much like the criminal legal system. For one thing, it deals with violations of the criminal law; for another, it can sanction the perpetrator by taking away his or her liberty and requiring him or her to pay fines. But strictly speaking, the juvenile court system is not part of the criminal law process. The basic difference is that perpetrators are children (legally, anyone under the age of 18), and because the law views children differently than adults, this affects the entire nature of the juvenile system.

Criminal conduct involves a criminal state of mind. But in medieval times, the church viewed children under the age of seven as naturally

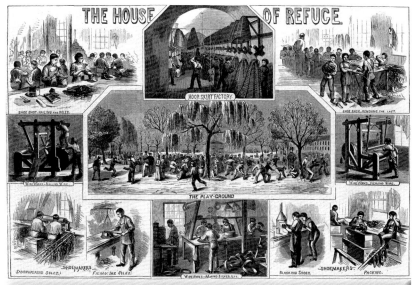

The New York House of Refuge, organized in 1816 and located on Randall's Island, was the first juvenile reformatory in the United States. *Corbis*

unable to commit sins because they could not fully understand the consequences of what they were doing (somewhat like the modern insanity defense). As the criminal law developed, this idea influenced courts so that they did not hold children of this age responsible for criminal actions. Children above the age of seven, however, were treated as if they were adults.

In the nineteenth century, society began to see childhood as a special phase of a person's life, a time during which children remained naturally innocent, emotionally as well as physically. As a result, social movements arose that began to seek special treatment for older children who engaged in criminal conduct. At first this involved sending them to work houses and reform schools instead of jails and prisons.

Later, as the Industrial Revolution gained ground in America, most people began to live in cities instead of the country. This meant that parents had workplaces outside the home, which disrupted the traditional family structure and functions. Because of this, reform movements began viewing government as a surrogate parent with the duty of making sure that the child had a proper environment in which to grow. (This is known as the doctrine of **parens patriae**, "the parent of the country," a phrase used by the Pennsylvania Supreme Court in Mary Ann Crouse's case.)

All of these developments led to the creation of the first juvenile court systems in the late 1800s and early 1900s. While these courts were designed to work somewhat like regular courts, they did have some major differences. The biggest, of course, was that they had jurisdiction in cases in which the individual was a child up to the age of 21 (later 18), not only for criminal conduct, but also for other matters such as child neglect or abuse. Another crucial difference was the goal of punishment. Unlike adult courts in which punishment could serve the purposes of deterrence, incapacitation, and retribution, the emphasis in juvenile court was on reform or rehabilitation. The major goal of the juvenile process was, and is, to act in the child's best interests and thus to provide a stable environment in which he or she can learn correct behavior and develop into a useful citizen.[2]

For this reason, juvenile courts use specialized terms. Instead of a criminal complaint, for instance, a juvenile proceeding often begins with a **petition** (which actually serves much the same purpose as the complaint.) Trials are called **adjudicatory hearings**, since unlike an adversarial trial, the idea is that all parties in the hearing (judge, lawyers, and family members) are engaged in seeking and acting in the child's best interests. A child who is found to have acted wrongly is declared to be a **delinquent** rather than convicted, and instead of being **sentenced**, his or her case receives **disposition**. Nevertheless, despite these different labels, the juvenile process bears strong similarity to the criminal process.

This similarity has greatly increased during the last half-century, for two reasons. First, society has begun to turn away from the nineteenth-century notion that children are naturally innocent and good. (An example of this is William Golding's violent portrayal of children in his 1954 novel *Lord of the Flies*.) Second, the United States Supreme Court decided, in a series of landmark cases of the 1960s and 1970s, that juveniles are entitled to several criminal procedural rights. As the court saw things, the juvenile system, which tended to be informal because all parties were theoretically acting in the child's best interests, could—because of this very informality—fail to protect children in the same way that the Bill of Rights protects the adult criminal defendant.

The leading case was *In re Gault*, which the Supreme Court decided in 1967. In that case, 15-year-old Gerald Francis Gault, who had already been in trouble with the law for being involved in a robbery, was accused by a neighbor of making obscene telephone calls. Police took Gault into custody and interrogated him for several hours without providing him an attorney or notifying his parents. When Gault appeared before a juvenile court judge, still without an attorney or being advised that he could remain silent, he admitted what he had done. Because Gault had been in trouble before, the judge ordered Gault to be confined in the state industrial school until he was 21—a period of more than six years. If Gault had been charged as an adult for making obscene phone calls, the maximum sentence could have been only a $50 fine. Obviously, something was very wrong with this system.

In the *Gault* decision the Supreme Court decided that juveniles, though not technically criminal defendants, were entitled to certain due process rights. Eventually in later cases, the court gave juveniles the privilege against self-incrimination, the right to an attorney, and the right to confront witnesses.[3]

As a result of *Gault* and later cases, then, the juvenile process has grown to resemble more strongly a criminal trial. While technically the goal of the juvenile process remains the reform of the child, in practice an element of punishment has also crept in, particularly when the criminal activity is serious.

THE JUVENILE JUSTICE PROCESS

A juvenile proceeding begins in much the same was as a regular criminal case. Someone may bring a juvenile's behavior to the authorities' attention, or police may discover the behavior on their own. A law officer may arrest a juvenile whom he or she suspects has committed a crime in the same way he or she may arrest an adult, and he or she is generally subject to the same limitations of probable cause and the same warrant requirements. But the arrest, search, and interrogation of juveniles differ in some important ways.

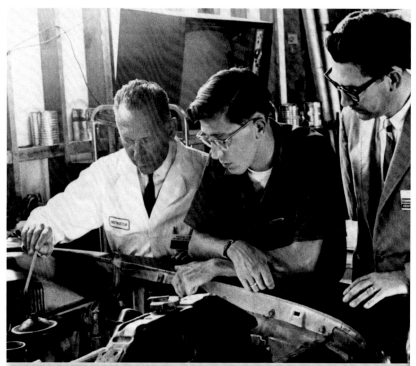

Gerald Gault, center, the Arizona youth whose appeal to the Supreme Court granted juveniles certain due process rights, studies automotive and heavy equipment operation at the Parks Job Corps Center in California in May 1967. *AP Photo/Ernest K. Bennett*

First, in addition to taking children into custody because of suspected crimes, law officers can also detain them for **status offenses**. These are offenses such as running away from home or failing to attend school, which are not criminal acts for adults. The idea of a status offense is that it somehow weakens or undermines the control of a parent or government that is necessary to ensure the child's welfare, supervision, and proper development.[4]

A second special case involves searches in schools by school officials. Because most children spend a great deal of time in school, and because teachers and other school employees need to ensure that the school is a safe and orderly environment, school officials may conduct reasonable searches of students and their lockers without warrants or probable cause.[5]

While in police custody, juveniles generally have the same *Miranda* rights as adults. Because children may not have the same understanding of these rights, however, police must take special care to ensure that a juvenile knows what he or she is doing if he or she waives these rights.[6]

When police take a child into custody, they normally notify the parents immediately and hold the child until their arrival. As they do in adult cases, police exercise a great deal of discretion at this phase. They may release the child to the parents with a warning, or in exchange for a promise to appear in juvenile court, or perhaps upon posting of station-house bail. If the crime in question is serious, however, police may continue to hold the child in a special detention area (not an adult jail) until his or her appearance in juvenile court, which must be within a day or two. If officers decide that juvenile court proceedings are the best option, then the case moves forward in the fashion described below.[7]

Intake

The beginning of the juvenile process is intake, which is managed by an intake officer. The police refer cases to the intake officer; other persons may also contact the intake officer as well. Anyone, including a juvenile's victim or even a child's parents, may ask an intake worker to investigate a juvenile problem. The intake worker, like the police, will then investigate the matter to decide whether court proceedings are the correct option.

During an intake conference, the intake officer will usually interview the child as well as his or her parents or guardians. Among other things, the officer tries to discover why the child acted as he or she did and whether he or she understood that his or her behavior was unlawful. The officer will also investigate whether the parents are likely to be able to correct such behavior in the future and whether the behavior is likely to happen again. While the child probably does not have a right to an attorney at this stage, some states may allow one to be present or require that a child be given a *Miranda* warning at this point.

The intake officer serves as a gatekeeper to the juvenile process, exercising great discretion as to which incidents require a full court proceeding and which ones may be **diverted** to more informal paths. In practice, intake workers divert about half the incidents that come before them into informal channels, such as drug or alcohol awareness educa-tion programs, family counseling, or educational activities or programs designed to build the child's self-esteem. Intake workers may also settle incidents by arranging for children to pay victims for any damage they may have caused. In less serious cases they may simply place the child on probation or even dismiss the case.

About half of all intake cases, however, are serious enough to require court involvement. In these cases, the intake officer files a petition with the juvenile court, which serves the same purpose as a criminal com-plaint in an adult court. Like a complaint, a petition must clearly state the facts of the case and the specific charges against the child.[8]

Detention

If police refer the child to an intake officer, then that officer and per-haps the judge must decide whether to continue to detain the child. In deciding whether to detain a juvenile, the intake worker usually consid-ers three elements: the likelihood that the child poses a danger to him or herself, the likelihood that the child is a danger to others, and the likelihood that the child will fail to appear in court. If the intake officer decides that detention is needed, the officer must file a petition with the court immediately. The decision then goes to the juvenile judge, who must decide within two or three days whether to detain the child. This decision usually takes place at a **detention hearing**, at which the child may be represented by a lawyer.[9]

A child may be held in several types of facility. The first option, **shel-ter care** or **outreach detention**, typically consists of detention within the parent or guardian's home. Court officers may closely supervise the child at home and even use electronic monitoring. The second option is a **detention facility**. Such a facility may be low security, such as a house without bars but with a staff that closely monitors the residents, or a secure facility, which resembles a prison although it is designed specifi-cally for the holding of juveniles.[10]

The law views detention of juveniles not only as preventing them from committing other crimes while they are waiting for trial, but also as a means of supervising them for their own good when parental supervision has failed. For these reasons, the Supreme Court has held that pretrial detention is allowed when the judge finds a serious risk that the child would commit more crimes if not detained.[11]

The Adjudicatory Hearing

The adjudicatory hearing is the juvenile court equivalent of a trial. It is the hearing at which the court decides, based on the evidence, whether or not the child committed the acts specified in the charges against him or her.

Before the *Gault* decision, the adjudicatory hearing, along with the entire juvenile system, was supposed to function as a social welfare process designed to work in the child's best interests. But the facts in *Gault* showed that in practice this was not always the case. As a result, the *Gault* court, in order to protect children, began to require that juvenile courts give children many of the same rights held by adult criminal defendants. The downside of this decision, however, was that because of *Gault* and later cases, the adjudicatory hearing became more adversarial and therefore more like an adult criminal trial.[12]

But the Supreme Court has not given children in juvenile court all of the rights of adult defendants. Instead, it does recognize, to an extent, that children stand in a special position to society and to the court. As a result, the adjudicatory hearing today shows a tension between the goal of acting in the child's best interests and the need to treat children as if they are criminal defendants.

In the wake of *Gault*, the adjudicatory hearing has much the same format as criminal trials. A state prosecutor submits evidence and summons and examines witnesses, which the child's attorney may cross-examine. The child's attorney may then introduce his or her own evidence and witnesses, and the prosecutor likewise may cross-examine them. The juvenile has the privilege against self-incrimination, and he or she also has a right to an attorney. One of the most striking similarities to the criminal process lies in the standard of proof: Prosecutors in juvenile cases must prove the charges beyond a reasonable doubt.[13]

The role of a child's lawyer in juvenile court is especially complex. Just as the juvenile process involves tension between the social welfare idea and the criminal trial idea, so, too, the lawyer in these proceeds finds him or herself in a difficult situation. Is his or her job to represent his or her client—the child—zealously in an adversarial fashion, as he or she would represent any adult criminal defendant? Or is he or she to assist the court in discovering the best way to act in the interests of the child? To complicate matters further, the child may be too young to understand these different approaches, or to be able to assist the lawyer in trying the case. Because of this, the child's lawyer may even be acting, in a sense, as the child's guardian for the purposes of the case.[14]

The most important difference between juvenile and criminal trials, as far as constitutional rights are concerned, is that juries are not required in juvenile cases. In *McKeiver v. Pennsylvania*, the United States Supreme Court found that the use of juries would make the juvenile process too adversarial. It would make the juvenile process too formal and inflexible, and it would also make them too public.[15]

Traditionally, juvenile hearings have been confidential in order to protect the welfare of the child; a jury would greatly reduce this confidentiality. In short, the Supreme Court said, the use of a jury would mean that juvenile hearings were practically no different from criminal trials, thus destroying the whole point of having a juvenile court system in the first place.[16]

After hearing all of the evidence, the judge decides the case. If he or she finds the child guilty—that is, an **adjudication of delinquency**—then the case moves on to the next phase. Otherwise the child is free to go.

The Disposition

If the court's declaration that a child is a delinquent is similar to a criminal court finding a defendant guilty, then disposition is similar to sentencing. But here, too, as in the other stages of the juvenile process, there are major differences in the approaches of juvenile and adult courts. The goal of disposition is to find a proper balance between the best interests of the child and the protection of society. In deciding how to deal with the delinquent, the judge does not focus so much on the criminal conduct involved as on the child's mental, emotional, and physical condition, with an eye toward helping the child avoid a downward spiral into a life of crime.

In order to help the judge reach the proper decision, the juvenile court staff prepares a **social history report**, also known as a **dispositional report**. This report may include an investigation of the child's prior juvenile record, his or her family and living arrangements, his or her school performance, his or her medical records, his or her religious background, his or her work history, and even evaluations by social workers, psychologists, and psychiatrists. All of this is designed to give the judge an understanding of the child's conditions—not only where he or she is, socially speaking, but also where he or she seems to be going.[17]

The judge then holds a dispositional hearing, at which he or she may hear testimony and review other evidence. Based on this information as well as the social history report, the judge then makes his or her decision. Because the goal is to see to the child's best interests, juvenile court judges have a wide range of options.

The most lenient and frequent option is probation. In fact, judges choose probation in more than half of the cases in which they find the children before them to be delinquent. As is the case in criminal court, the basic idea of probation is a requirement of good behavior. Probation usually lasts from one to three years. During this time, the child usually lives at home with parents or with other near relatives and continues to attend school. The judge may require the child to meet regularly with a probation officer, and he or she may impose other requirements as well. Some of these requirements may be curfews, community service, a ban on driving, random drug and alcohol testing, substance abuse treatment, or psychological counseling. Judges may even prohibit the child from watching television if he or she has decided that television has contributed to the child's behavior. An important condition is the requirement that the child pay the victim for any damage he or she caused. If, during his or her probation, the child fails to meet the conditions that the judge has set forth, or if he or she commits another crime, the judge may revoke the probation and impose another, harsher, disposition.[18]

A step up from probation is out-of-home placement, which the court may require when the parents or near relatives are either unable or unwilling to supervise the child properly. This step involves placing the child in a foster home or in a group home where he or she will be under close supervision. Judges may also combine out-of-home placement with some of the conditions of probation.[19]

A more extreme step is institutional confinement. Here the child is placed in a special facility, usually operated by the government, which involves very close supervision, confinement, and a set daily schedule. There is a wide range of such institutions nationwide, with different options varying by state. Some of these institutions are work camps or ranches, while others are training or industrial schools where the emphasis is on educating the child. The most restrictive institutions closely resemble prisons with the major difference being that the only residents are juveniles. One recent development is the boot camp, which is based on a military-style model of very intensive "shock" training.[20]

The current system of juvenile justice has received a great deal of criticism. Originally designed as a social welfare procedure, it often failed to protect child offenders from unjust punishments. The Supreme Court's remedy to this problem in *Gault* and other key cases was to give juveniles due process protections, but this led to the juvenile courts becoming more like adult criminal courts, which the juvenile system was originally supposed to avoid.

Today, the juvenile system is a strange mix of social welfare program and criminal court. While it is supposed to act in the child's best interest, in practical terms, it often emphasizes punishment instead. How the system will develop in the future remains to be seen.

NO PERFECT ANSWERS

The juvenile justice system is based on the idea that children—somewhat like adults who use the insanity defense—are not entirely aware of the consequences of their actions, or who, like those under duress or who plead necessity, are not acting entirely out of their own free will because of the pressures of their circumstances. But what about older children near the age of 18 who have repeatedly committed crimes, or who have carried out one or more particularly violent crimes? What if all the resources of the juvenile process have failed to reform a delinquent?

In cases such as these, the decision may be made to try the juvenile in regular court as an adult. Depending on the state, this decision may be up to the juvenile court judge, the prosecutor, or even the state legislature, which may require that juveniles who commit major crimes to be treated as adults.

When this happens, juveniles have their cases heard by regular courts. They have the full range of criminal procedural rights that they would not have had in juvenile courts, including the right to trial by jury. On the other hand, if they are convicted, they will be subject to the same sentences as adults, including such extreme punishments as life imprisonment or even the death penalty.[21]

The key word here is "punishment." While rehabilitation or reform is one of the possible goals of the criminal justice system, most of the goals involve making the criminal pay for his or her crime, or else preventing him or her (or discouraging other would-be criminals) from committing crimes in the future. These are very different goals from the main ones sought by the juvenile system.

The decision to treat certain juveniles as adults, then, comes back full circle to the issue with which this book began: why criminal conduct is punished. If society believes that some juveniles may not be responsible for their actions while others are, it even raises questions of free will, as in cases of sleepwalking, duress, and insanity.

Depending on the particular case, there may be no perfect answer to some of these issues. In the end, the *Dudley* case and its grisly episode of cannibalism at sea remains a useful illustration. Most people would agree that Dudley and Stephens acted wrongly, but the question still remains as to whether, why, and how they should have been punished for those actions. While the *Dudley* trial is long past, criminal courts today still face those basic questions in every case they hear.

Endnotes

Chapter 1

1. A. W. Brian Simpson, *Cannibalism and the Common Law: The Story of the Last Voyage of the Mignonette and the Strange Legal Proceedings to Which It Gave Rise* (Chicago: University of Chicago Press, 1984), 30, 42.
2. *Ibid.*, 46–49.
3. *Ibid.*, 55–68.
4. *Ibid.*, 76–79, 241–42.
5. Marcus Tullius Cicero, *De Officiis*, Walter Miller, trans. (London: William Heinemann, 1921), ix; book 3, 23, 363–65.
6. Simpson, *Cannibalism and the Common Law*, 239.
7. Cf. Lon L. Fuller, "The Case of the Speluncean Explorers," *Harvard Law Review* 62 (1949): 616.
8. Bruce Nash, *Lawyer's Wit and Wisdom* (Philadelphia: Running Press, 1995), 152; cf. Oliver Wendell Holmes, Jr., *Justice Holmes to Doctor Wu: An Intimate Correspondence, 1921–1932* (New York: Central Book Co., 1947), 53.
9. *Northern Sec. Co. v. United States*, 193 U.S. 197, 400 (1904) (Holmes, J., dissenting).

Chapter 2

1. Gerald F. Uelman, *The O. J. Files: Evidentiary Issues in a Tactical Context* (St. Paul: West Group Publishing, 1997), 40–42.
2. Michael Fleeman, "O. J. Leads Cops on Chase Hunt Ends with Surrender at Home," *Chicago Sun-Times*, June 18, 1994; Brian McGrory, "Chronology; From Morning of Shocks to Nighttime Surrender; O. J. Simpson: Sports Legend Under Arrest," *Boston Globe*, June 19, 1994. *See generally* Vincent Bugliosi, *Outrage: The Five Reasons Why O. J. Simpson Got Away with Murder* (New York: W. W. Norton & Co., 2008).
3. William Blackstone, *Commentaries on the Laws of England*, vol. 2 (Oxford: Clarendon Press, 1766), 352.
4. *The Code of Hammurabi, King of Babylon about 2250 B.C.*, Robert Francis Harper, trans. (Chicago: The University of Chicago Press, 1904), 17–19, 21–22.
5. William Stubbs, *Select Charters and Other Illustrations of English Constitutional History: From the Earliest Times to the Reign of Edward the First*, 8th ed. (Oxford: Clarendon Press, 1905), 65–66.
6. *Simpson v. Brown*, 67 Cal. App. 4th 914, 79 Cal. Rptr. 2d 389 (1998).
7. *People v. Simpson*, No. BA097211 (Cal. Super. Ct. L.A. County Oct. 3, 1995).

Chapter 3

1. "Conference on the 30th Anniversary of the United States Supreme Court's Decision in Gideon v. Wainwright: *Gideon* and the Public Service Role of Lawyers in Advancing Equal Justice," *American University Law Review* 43 (1993): 1, 34.
2. *Ibid.*, 35.
3. *Ibid.*, 42.
4. U.S. Constitution, art. 1, sec. 8.
5. Kathleen Maguire et. al, ed., *Sourcebook of Criminal Justice Statistics 2003* (Washington: Government Printing Office, 2005), 418, table 5.17; 449, table 5.44.
6. U.S. Constitution, art. 1, sec. 9, cl. 3; *ibid.*, art. 1, sec. 10, cl. 1; *ibid.*, art. 1, sec. 9, cl. 2.
7. Henry J. Abraham, and Barbara A. Perry, *Freedom and the Court: Civil Rights and Liberties in the United States* (Lawrence: University Press of Kansas, 2003).
8. *Malloy v. Hogan*, 378 U.S. 1 (1964); *Benton v. Maryland*, 395 U.S. 784 (1969); *Duncan v. Louisiana*, 391 U.S. 145 (1968).
9. *Hurtado v. California*, 110 U.S. 516 (1884); *Murphy v. Hunt*, 455 U.S. 478 (1982).

Chapter 4

1. Ernest Kahlar Alix, *Ransom Kidnapping in America, 1874–1974: The Creation of a Capital Crime* (Carbondale: Southern Illinois University Press, 1978); Christian Ross, *The Father's Story of Charley Ross, the Kidnapped Child* (Philadelphia: John E. Potter & Co., 1876).
2. Horace L. Bomar, Jr., "The Lindbergh Law," *Law & Contemporary Problems* 1 (1934): 435; Robert

C. Finley, "The Lindbergh Law," *Georgetown Law Journal* 28 (1940): 908.
3. Bomar, "The Lindbergh Law," 436.
4. *Ibid.*, 437.
5. Finley, "The Lindbergh Law," 913–15.
6. Adam Clymer, "In House and Senate, 2 Kinds of G.O.P.," *New York Times*, November 15, 1994.
7. Linda Greenhouse, "The New, Improved (?) Filibuster in Action," *New York Times*, May 21, 1987.
8. Walter J. Oleszek, *Congressional Procedures and the Policy Process*, 6th ed. (Washington: CQ Press, 2004), 20–21.
9. Alan Rosenthal, *The Third House: Lobbyists and Lobbying in the States* (Washington: CQ Press, 2001).
10. Oleszek, *Congressional Procedures and the Policy Process*, 76.
11. Jack Davies, *Legislative Law and Process in a Nutshell* (St. Paul: West Publishing Co., 1975), 95–109.
12. *Ibid.*, 30–36.
13. Oleszek, *Congressional Procedures and the Policy Process*, 175–77.
14. Davies, *Legislative Law and Process in a Nutshell*, 40–43.
15. U.S. Constitution, art. 1, sec. 7; Zoe Davis, comp., *Presidential Vetoes, 1789-2000*, S. Pub 107-10 (Washington, D.C.: Government Printing Office, 2001), viii–ix.
16. U.S. Constitution, art. 1, sec. 7; *Wright v. United States*, 302 U.S. 583 (1938); *Presidential Vetoes, 1789-2000*, viii–ix.

Chapter 5

1. *State v. Rider*, 90 Mo. 54, 1 S.W. 825 (1886); *State v. Rider*, 95 Mo. 474, 8 S.W. 723 (1888).

2. Wayne R. LaFave, *Criminal Law*, 3d ed. (St. Paul: West Group, 2000), 207–08, 224–25, 283–86.

3. *Model Penal Code and Commentaries* (Official Draft and Revised Comments) sec. 2.02(1), 2.02(2) (1985); LaFave, *Criminal Law*, 229–34.

4. *Model Penal Code and Commentaries* (Official Draft and Revised Comments) sec. 2.02(2) (1985); LaFave, *Criminal Law*, 246–56.

5. *Model Penal Code and Commentaries* (Official Draft and Revised Comments) sec. 2.05 (1985); LaFave, *Criminal Law*, 257–83.

6. *Smith v. State*, 284 Ga. 33, 663 S.E. 2d 155 (2008); *People v. Brand*, 13 A.D.3d 820, 787 N.Y.S.2d 169 (2004).

7. *Martin v. State*, 31 Ala. App. 334, 17 So. 2d 427 (1944).

8. LaFave, *Criminal Law*, 567–86.

9. *Ibid.*, sec. 3.3.

10. *Ibid.*, sec. 3.12.

11. *Ibid.*

12. *Ibid.*, sec. 5.7–5.9; *State v. Rider*, 90 Mo. 54, 1 S.W. 825 (1886).

13. LaFave, *Criminal Law*, sec. 5.5.

14. *Ibid.*, sec. 5.4.

15. *Ibid.*, sec. 5.3.

16. *Ibid.*, sec. 5.2.

17. *Ibid.*, sec. 5.1.

18. Robert V. Remini, *Andrew Jackson and the Course of American Empire, 1767–1821* (New York: Harper & Row, 1977), ch. 5.

19. LaFave, *Criminal Law*, sec. 4.11.

20. *Ibid.*, sec. 4.10; *ibid.*, p. 416.

21. *M'Naghten's Case*, 8 Eng. Rep. 718 (1843).

22. *Parsons v. State*, 2 So. 854, 863–64, 866–67 (Ala. 1887).

23. *Model Penal Code and Commentaries* (Official Draft and Revised Comments) sec. 4.01(l) (1985).

24. *State v. Rider*, 95 Mo. 474, 8 S.W. 723 (1888); Diary of Wilbert S. Myers, July 13, 1888, Ancestry.com, http://freepages.genealogy.rootsweb.ancestry.com/~meredythspages/diary1888.htm (Accessed September 29, 2009).

Chapter 6

1. *Miranda v. Arizona*, 384 U.S. 436 (1966).

2. Wayne R. LaFave, Jerold H. Israel, and Nancy J. King, *Criminal Procedure*, 3d ed. (St. Paul: West Group, 2000), 8–12.

3. Radley Balko, *Overkill: The Rise of Paramilitary Police Raids in America* (Washington: Cato Institute, 2006), 43–63.

4. Charles H. Whitebread and Christopher Slobogin, *Criminal Procedure: An Analysis of Cases and Concepts*, 4th ed. (New York: Foundation Press, 2000), sec. 4.05.

5. *Katz v. United States*, 389 U.S. 347, 351 (1967).

6. Whitebread and Slobogin, *Criminal Procedure*, sec. 5.03; *Brinegar v. United States*, 338 U.S. 160, 175 (1949).

7. Whitebread and Slobogin, *Criminal Procedure*, sec. 5.04(b).

8. LaFave, Israel, and King, *Criminal Procedure*, 172–73; *Richards v. Wisconsin*, 520 U.S. 385 (1997).

9. Whitebread and Slobogin, *Criminal Procedure*, chaps. 6–12.

10. *Ibid.*, 47.

11. LaFave, Israel, and King, *Criminal Procedure*, 113–15; *Mapp v. Ohio*, 367 U.S. 643, 657–60 (1961).

12. Whitebread and Slobogin, *Criminal Procedure*, chap. 15.

13. *Rochin v. California*, 342 U.S. 165 (1952); Whitebread and Slobogin, *Criminal Procedure*, sec. 17.04.

14. *Escobedo v. Illinois*, 378 U.S. 478, 492 (1964).

15. Whitebread and Slobogin, *Criminal Procedure*, chap. 23.

16. *Ibid.*, 600.

Chapter 7

1. *Ex parte* Duncan, 66 F. Supp. 976 (D. Haw. 1944); *Ex parte* Duncan, 146 F.2d 576 (9th Cir. 1944); *Duncan v. Kahanamoku*, 327 U.S. 304 (1946).

2. LaFave, Israel, and King, *Criminal Procedure*, sec. 1.4(c).

3. *Ibid.*, 13–15.

4. U.S. Constitution, art. 1, sec. 9; Robert Searles Walker, *Habeas Corpus Writ of Liberty: English and American Origins and Development* (North Charleston, S.C.: Book-Surge Publishing, 2006); William F. Duker, *A Constitutional History of Habeas Corpus* (Westport, Conn.: Greenwood Press, 1980).

5. LaFave, Israel, and King, *Criminal Procedure*, 637–43.

6. *Ibid.*, 18–19; Whitebread and Slobogin, *Criminal Procedure*, chap. 22.

7. *Ibid.*, 20.

8. *Ibid.*, 21.

9. *Ibid.*, 956–58.

10. Paul Bergman, *Trial Advocacy in a Nutshell* (St. Paul: West Publishing Co., 1979), 250.

11. Edward J. Imwinkelried et al., *Courtroom Criminal Evidence*, vol. 1 (Newark: Matthew Bender, 2005), sec. 102.

12. *Federal Rules of Evidence* (St. Paul: West Group, 2008).

13. Whitebread and Slobogin, *Criminal Procedure*, chap. 25; LaFave, Israel, and King, *Criminal Procedure*, 22.

14. Whitebread and Slobogin, *Criminal Procedure*, chap. 28.

15. Imwinkelried et al., *Courtroom Criminal Evidence*, chap.1, sec. 101.

16. *Ibid.*, sec. 129.

17. *Ibid.*, sec. 102.

18. Bergman, *Trial Advocacy in a Nutshell*, chap. 5; LaFave, Israel, and King, *Criminal Procedure*, 1130–31.

19. LaFave, Israel, and King, *Criminal Procedure*, sec. 24.8.

20. *Ibid.*, 1128–29.

21. *Ibid.*, 1025–26.

22. Whitebread and Slobogin, *Criminal Procedure*, chap. 30.

23. *Ibid.*, chap. 33; LaFave, Israel, and King, *Criminal Procedure*, 25, 1292–1349.

Chapter 8

1. *Ex parte Crouse*, 4 Whart. 9 (Pa. 1839); Thomas J. Bernard, *The Cycle of Juvenile Justice* (New York: Oxford University Press, 1992), 68.

2. Barry C. Feld, *Juvenile Justice Administration in a Nutshell* (St. Paul: West Group, 2003), 2–8.

3. *In re Gault*, 387 U.S. 1 (1967); *In re Winship*, 397 U.S. 358 (1970); *McKeiver v. Pennsylvania*, 403 U.S. 528 (1971).

4. Feld, *Juvenile Justice Administration*, 40–50.

5. Mary J. Clement, *The Juvenile Justice System: Law and Process*, 2d ed. (Boston: Butterworth-Heinemann, 2002), 118–19; *New Jersey v. T. L. O.*, 469 U.S. 325 (1985).

6. Clement, *Juvenile Justice System*, 120–27.

7. Hazel B. Kerper, *Introduction to the Criminal Justice System*, 2d ed. (St. Paul: West Publishing Company, 1979), 393–94; Clement, *Juvenile Justice System*, 132–34.

8. Clement, *Juvenile Justice System*, 134–38; Feld, *Juvenile Justice Administration*, 142–55.

9. Feld, *Juvenile Justice Administration*, 156–59, 168–71.

10. Clement, *Juvenile Justice System*, 139–40; Feld, *Juvenile Justice Administration*, 157–58.

11. Feld, *Juvenile Justice Administration*, 162–65.

12. *Ibid.*, 229.

13. *In re Winship*, 397 U.S. 358 (1970).

14. Feld, *Juvenile Justice Administration*, 284.

15. *McKeiver v. Pennsylvania*, 403 U.S. 528 (1971).

16. Feld, *Juvenile Justice Administration*, 236–41.

17. *Ibid.*, 305–06; Kerper, *Introduction to the Criminal Justice System*, 396–97.

18. Feld, *Juvenile Justice Administration*, 341–42, 344–46; Clement, *Juvenile Justice System*, 135.

19. Feld, *Juvenile Justice Administration*, 348–49.

20. Clement, *Juvenile Justice System*, 173, 198–203; Feld, *Juvenile Justice Administration*, 349–54.

21. Feld, *Juvenile Justice Administration*, ch. 6.

Glossary

acquittal   A judge's or jury's declaration that a criminal defendant is not guilty of a crime

act   a bill that has completed the legislative process and become a law

actus reus   A "guilty act" that makes a person guilty of criminal conduct when combined with a criminal state of mind; see *mens rea*

adjudication of delinquency   A juvenile court's decision that a child has violated a criminal law or engaged in disobedient, indecent, or immoral conduct

adjudicatory hearing   A hearing in juvenile court that resembles an adult criminal trial

administrative regulations   Regulations set forth by an administrative agency that enable it to carry out that agency's legal powers and duties

adversarial system   A legal system in which one party contends with another to reach a favorable outcome for himself, with the judge acting as an independent referee

affirmance   An appellate court's decision to uphold the decision of the court below

amendment   An addition or modification; the United States Constitution has 27 amendments. See *Bill of Rights*

appeal   A complaint to an appellate court by a party to a case that the court below has made a legal error

appellate court   A court that reviews decisions of lower courts

arraignment   A hearing in which a court informs the defendant of the charges against him or her, to which the defendant is asked to plead "guilty," "not guilty," or "not guilty by reason of insanity"

assistance of counsel   A defendant's right to the assistance of a lawyer in presenting his or her case in a criminal trial, guaranteed by the Sixth Amendment

automobile exception   A legal doctrine that allows police to search vehicles for evidence of a crime without a warrant if they have probable cause

bail   Money required from a person charged with a crime in exchange for his or her release from custody as a means of guaranteeing that he or she will appear in court for his trial

bench trial   A trial held by a judge without the presence of a jury

beyond a reasonable doubt   The standard of proof that the prosecution must meet in criminal cases to convict a defendant of a crime; under this standard the proof of guilt is so certain that a reasonable person could not doubt it; see presumption of innocence; reasonable doubt

bicameralism   The division of a legislature into two chambers, or houses

bill   A proposed new law, or change to an existing law, that a legislature is formally considering.

bill of attainder   A legislative act that punishes a person without a court trial

Bill of Rights   In American law, the first ten amendments to the United States Constitution; also, a declaration of rights and liberties that may be found in various state constitutions

binding over   The transfer of a case from a magistrate to a grand jury or a criminal trial court after a finding of probable cause to believe that the defendant committed a crime

canon law   A body of law developed by the Catholic Church during the Middle Ages

capacity defense   A defendant's claim that he or she lacked responsibility or accountability necessary for him or her to be guilty of a crime

capital offense   A crime for which the death penalty may be imposed

case law   Law that is found in a collection of court cases and the principles that these cases set forth; see *common law*

causation   The relationship between a cause and an effect; see cause in fact and proximate cause

cause in fact   An act, omission, or circumstance that causes a certain result which would not have happened otherwise

challenge   See *jury challenge*

charge   The specific crime that a person is accused of committing; see also jury charge

civil trial   A trial of a civil case, involving either private or public parties, in which only civil penalties and not criminal punishments are possible

closing argument   The final statement by an attorney to a judge or jury summarizing the evidence he or she has presented in a trial

cloture   A legislative rule that ends a filibuster and allows a vote on a law or other measure to take place

code   A systematic collection of laws, rules, or regulations, often organized by subject

common law   A set of legal principles and rules based on the age-old custom of the community, recognized by and set forth in judicial decisions; common law forms a major basis of the English and American legal systems; see *custom*

complaint   In criminal law, a charge before a judge or magistrate that a person has committed a particular criminal offense

compulsory process   The authority to compel a witness's attendance and testimony at court; the Sixth Amendment gives this right to all criminal defendants

conference committee   A committee of members from both houses of a legislature, which is charged with resolving the differences between the two houses on a proposed statute; see bicameralism

confrontation of witnesses   A criminal defendant's Sixth Amendment right to meet witnesses face-to-face in court and challenge their testimony by cross-examination

conspiracy   A crime in which two or more persons agree to commit an illegal act and take some substantial step towards committing it

constitution   The foundational law of a state or nation that sets forth the government's basic structure and powers along with individuals' fundamental rights; all other laws of the state or nation must conform to the constitution

contempt of court   An action designed to interfere with a court's administration of justice, its authority, or its dignity; courts may punish a person who is in contempt by fines or imprisonment

conviction   A verdict or judgment in a criminal case that the defendant is guilty of a criminal charge

Corpus Juris Civilis   The body of Roman civil law assembled and organized during the reign of the Emperor Justinian in the sixth century

credibility   The issue of whether a witness is reliable and whether his or her statements are therefore worthy of belief

crime   A specific type of conduct that violates a person's duties to society and which is punishable by imprisonment, death, or fines

criminal complaint   See *complaint*

criminal law   The rules of law, designed for society's protection, that declare what conduct is criminal and sets forth the punishments for such conduct

criminal procedure   The rules of law governing how crimes are investigated, tried, and punished

criminal trial   A trial prosecuted by the government in which criminal punishments, such as imprisonment, execution, and criminal fines, are possible

cross-examination   The examination of a witness by the opposing party with the goal of testing the truth of his or her testimony

custom   A traditional course of action that is repeated in similar circumstances; see *Common law*

delinquent   A child who has violated a criminal law or engaged in disobedient, indecent, or immoral conduct

detention   Restraining another's freedom of movement; police officers detain individuals when they hold them for questioning; juveniles are often detained prior to the filing of a petition in juvenile court or after an adjudication of delinquency

detention facility   A facility for holding juvenile delinquents under supervision

detention hearing   A court hearing to determine whether detention of a juvenile or some other person is proper

deterrence   A purpose of criminal punishment. Deterrence prevents or discourages persons, either the criminal or members of the general population, from committing crimes

direct examination   An examination of a witness, by the party who has called him or her to testify, regarding the charge against a defendant

disposition   In juvenile court, the judge's decision regarding the delinquency of the child in question and the actions, if any, he or she requires of the child

dispositional report   A report on a juvenile delinquent's mental and physical health as well as his or her family and social circumstances, which the juvenile judge uses to decide on how to deal with the child's case

diversion   In juvenile court, a decision by an intake worker or judge to channel a child into an educational, training, or reform program instead of holding an adjudicatory hearing

double jeopardy   A Fifth Amendment right that prohibits a government from prosecuting the same person more than once for the same offense

due process of law   The concept that government, when exercising its power, must do so in accord with established laws and procedures and with respect for the established rights of individuals and groups; the notion that government itself must obey the law; in criminal law, due process includes the requirement that the defendant receive a fair trial and is entitled to the presumption of innocence, in addition to having the protections listed in the Bill of Rights

duress   A criminal defense that states that a defendant is not guilty of a crime because he or she was acting under some coercion or threat by another person

empanelling   The selection of a set of jurors for the trial of a particular case

entrapment   A criminal defense that states that law officers encouraged or tempted a defendant to commit a crime that he or she would not otherwise have committed

evanescent evidence   Evidence that is likely to vanish or cease to exist within a short time, such as a person's blood alcohol level

ex post facto **law**   A law that criminalizes actions taking place before the law's passage

exclusionary rule   A rule that prohibits the use of evidence that the government obtained as the result of an illegal search or seizure

excuse   A legal defense in which a defendant shows a legal justification for conduct that would otherwise be criminal

expert witnesses   A witness who has knowledge of a subject superior to other persons because of his or her education or experience

federalism   The division of power between the state governments on the one hand and the national, or federal, government on the other

felony   A major criminal offense that traditionally involves capital punishment or imprisonment for more than one year

filibuster   A protracted debate, typically in the United States Senate, designed to delay and obstruct the passage of legislation; see *cloture*

first appearance   An initial court appearance shortly after a suspect's arrest, in which a magistrate informs a suspect of the charges against him or her, advises him or her of his or her *Miranda* rights, and sets bail

fruit of the poisonous tree A legal doctrine that prevents the use of evidence that police obtained legally if they obtained it because of a previous illegal search or seizure

grand jury A jury of inquiry, which has the power and duty to hear complaints of criminal activity, investigate possible crimes, and accuse suspects of having engaged in criminal conduct; see *indictment*; *presentment*.

habeas corpus A writ, or court order, to someone who detains another, requiring him or her to show legal cause for the detention

hearsay rule A rule that bars the testimony of a witness about what he or she has heard others say

homicide The killing of one human being by the act or omission of another; homicide includes the crimes of murder and manslaughter, but it also includes noncriminal killings such as killing in self-defense, execution of criminals, and police killings of suspects by the legal use of deadly force

hypothetical question A question about a fictional set of events designed to analyze the legal rules involved

incapacitation A purpose of criminal punishment; an action to prevent the perpetrator of a crime from committing other crimes in the future; execution is the most extreme method of incapacitation

Incorporation of the Bill of Rights The United States Supreme Court's extension of the guarantees of the federal Bill of Rights to cases in state courts by incorporating them into the Due Process Clause of the Fourteenth Amendment; see *federalism*

indictment A formal written accusation by a grand jury that a particular person has committed a specific criminal offense, based on an initial charge by a prosecutor; see also *information*; *presentment*

information A written accusation by a prosecutor or other public official, without the use of a grand jury, that a particular person has committed a specific criminal offense; see also *indictment*; *presentment*

insanity A legal defense that claims that the defendant is not guilty because did not know the nature and consequence of his or her acts or could not control his or her behavior; see *M'Naghten rule*

intake The first step in the juvenile process, during which an intake officer studies the facts and background of the case and decides whether to dismiss or divert the case or to proceed to adjudication

intent A state of mind in which a person seeks to bring about a particular result by a course of action; see *mens rea*

interpretation The process of discovering or ascertaining the meaning of a constitutional phrase, a statute, or some other legal language

jurisdiction "To speak the law"; the legal authority of a particular court to hear and decide a case, based on the parties involved, the subject matter of a case, or a geographical region

jury challenge A party's request that a judge disqualify a juror in order to ensure an unbiased or favorable jury

jury charge   1. A judge's address to a grand jury in which he or she instructs the jury as to its duties; 2. A final address by a judge to a trial jury in which he or she instructs the jury as to the rules of law that apply to the issues in the case

justification   See *excuse*

juvenile court   A court having jurisdiction of a parental nature over delinquent children

knowledge   A state of mind in which a person is aware of the nature of his or her conduct and that the conduct is practically certain to bring about a certain result; see *mens rea*

leading question   A question to a witness that suggests a particular answer or puts words in the witness's mouth

legal cause   See *proximate cause*

Leges Barbarorum   Medieval codes of law that codified the customs of the Germanic tribes

liability without fault   An exception to the rule that criminal liability requires a criminal state of mind; liability without fault only applies in minor regulatory offenses where proof of a state of mind would be practically impossible

lobbyist   One who is engaged in the business of, or who has a special interest in, persuading legislators to vote in a certain way or to introduce certain legislation

magistrate   A minor judicial officer who has the authority to issue warrants, review arrests, set bail, and carry out some other judicial functions

Magna Carta   A foundational document of Anglo-American legal history, written in 1215, that includes an early version of due process of law

manslaughter   A type of homicide committed without intent, or under the influence of some extreme mental or emotional disturbance, which makes the crime less blameworthy than murder

mens rea   A "guilty mind," a criminal mental state that makes a person guilty of criminal conduct when combined with a wrongful act; the Model Penal Code sets forth four levels of *mens rea*: intent, knowledge, recklessness, and negligence; see *actus reus*.

Miranda **rights**   Basic rights that law officers must make sure criminal suspects are acquainted before interrogation, including the privilege against self-incrimination ("You have the right to remain silent,") and the right to assistance of counsel; the Supreme Court set forth this requirement in *Miranda v. Arizona*

Misdemeanor   A relatively minor criminal offense that traditionally involves only the payment of a fine, imprisonment for less than one year, or both

mistake   A situation in which a person, because of an erroneous idea about facts or legal duties, acts in a way that he or she would not have acted otherwise. Some mistakes are legal defenses to criminal charges

M'Naghten rule   The basic rule for determining whether a person charged with a crime is legally insane; it asks whether the perpetrator "was labouring under such a defect of reason, from disease of the mind, as not to know the nature and quality of the act he or she was doing, or as not to know that what he or she was doing was wrong"; see *insanity*

Model Penal Code   A criminal law code compiled by legal scholars to serve as a guide for national and state lawmakers

murder   A homicide which the perpetrator committed intentionally or knowingly, or with a recklessness showing extreme indifference to human life

natural law   A set of universal rules for human conduct that exists independently of any legal system and knowable by human reason

necessity   A defense to a criminal charge in which the circumstances require a perpetrator to act as he or she does in order to preserve his or her life or health

negligence   A state of mind in which a person is aware of the nature of his conduct and that the conduct is practically certain to bring about a certain result; see *mens rea*

omission   A failure to act in a way that the law requires; an omission can be an *actus reus*

outreach detention   See *shelter care*

override   A supermajority vote of a legislature that enacts a vetoed bill into law

parens patriae   "Parent of the country"; the doctrine that the government may act as the guardian of children or others who are under a legal disability

parliamentary procedure   The rules that govern the procedure of a legislature for passing laws or conducting other business

petition   A request that begins juvenile court review of an action involving a child; the juvenile court version of a criminal complaint

petit jury   See *trial jury*

plaintiff   The party who initiates or begins a civil lawsuit

plain view   A doctrine that allows police to seize illegal goods that are in plain view during a lawful search even though the police do not have a warrant to search for those goods

plea bargaining   The process of negotiation between a prosecutor and a criminal defendant in which the defendant agrees to plead guilty in exchange for concessions from the prosecutor

pocket veto   A veto of a bill that occurs when a chief executive fails to sign it before the end of the legislative session

precedent   In common law jurisdictions, a judicial decision that provides a legal rule for a court to follow in similar future cases

predisposition   In the entrapment defense, a defendant's inclination to act in a certain way even before being tempted by law officers to commit a crime

preliminary hearing   A hearing held before a criminal trial in which a magistrate or judge requires the prosecutor to show that probable cause exists to believe that the defendant has committed a crime

preponderance of the evidence   A standard of proof in civil (not criminal) trials in which a party, in order to win, must prove that his case is more likely than not

presentment   A formal accusation of a crime by a grand jury based on its own investigation; see *indictment; information*

presumption of innocence   A principle of due process and criminal law that declares a criminal defendant to be innocent until the prosecutor has produced evidence to show that he is guilty beyond a reasonable doubt

privilege against self-incrimination   The Fifth Amendment guarantee that a criminal defendant has the right not to be a witness against him or herself; see *Miranda rights*

probable cause   A reasonable ground for belief in certain facts that is necessary for legal police searches, seizures, and arrests, as well as for a filing of formal charges against a defendant

probation   A criminal sentence or a juvenile court disposition that releases a person back into the community, subject to supervision and conditions of behavior, instead of imprisoning him or her

prosecutor   A government attorney who files charges in criminal cases, guides grand jury investigations, and presents the government case against a criminal defendant

proximate cause   Conduct that produces an injury without any intervening causes

public defender   A lawyer who is paid by the government to defend persons accused of crimes who cannot afford to pay lawyers themselves

public trial   A nonsecret trial that the public is free to attend; guaranteed in all criminal cases by the Sixth Amendment

real evidence   Evidence furnished by things rather than by witness testimony about or descriptions of things

reasonable doubt   A doubt that is based on reason and evidence or the lack of evidence, rather than on imagination or fancy; see beyond a reasonable doubt; presumption of innocence

rebuttal   A stage in a criminal trial in which a prosecutor presents evidence to explain or disprove facts and evidence submitted by the defendant

recklessness   A state of mind in which a person is aware of the nature of his or her conduct and that the conduct is likely to bring about a certain result; see *mens rea*

re-cross examination   An examination of a witness by the cross-examiner after the re-direct examination

re-direct examination   An examination of a witness by the direct examiner after the cross-examination

reform/education   A purpose of criminal punishment. Reform seeks to teach the criminal the wrongful nature of his or her criminal conduct and to help him or her learn behavior that will allow him or her to avoid such conduct in the future; reform is a major goal in the juvenile justice system

rejoinder   A stage in a criminal trial in which a defendant presents evidence to explain or disprove facts and evidence submitted by the prosecutor during the rebuttal

relevance   A rule of evidence that requires the evidence in a case show that a fact important to the outcome of a case be more or less likely

remand   To send back; an appellate court may remand a case to the trial court, or a judge may remand a prisoner rather than allow him or her to go free on bail

retribution   A purpose of criminal punishment. Retribution is based on the idea of revenge and the notion that every perpetrator of a crime must pay somehow for having committed that crime

reversal   An appellate court's decision to reverse the decision of the court below in order to achieve the opposite outcome

rules of evidence   Rules that control the type of evidence that the parties to a trial may introduce, as well as how they use that evidence

search incident to lawful arrest   A doctrine that allows a police officer to make a warrantless search of a suspect whom he has legally arrested

self-defense   A defense to a criminal charge in which the circumstances permit a perpetrator to use force against another person in order to preserve his or her own life or safety, or the safety of his property

sentencing   A judge's or jury's decision as to the punishment that will be imposed on a convicted criminal

separation of powers   The division of executive, legislative, and judicial powers among three separate branches of government as a way of avoiding the danger of one individual or group exercising a dangerous amount of power

shelter care   Detention of a juvenile within the parent or guardian's home. Court officers may closely supervise the child at home and even use electronic monitoring

social history report   A report prepared by the staff of a juvenile court analyzing the social, psychological, medical, and financial conditions of a juvenile delinquent in order to help the judge decide on a proper disposition

speedy trial   A right of defendants in all criminal cases, granted by the Sixth Amendment, to receive a trial without unreasonable delay

state   A sovereign government, which possesses legislative, executive, and judicial branches; see *federalism*

station-house bail   Bail that is set by law for relatively minor crimes and may be arranged at a police station without the involvement of a magistrate

status offense   An offense based not on a child's action but on his or her character as a child needing supervision

statute   A formal written law set forth by a legislature

strict liability crime   A crime that does not require a criminal mental state; strict liability crimes are limited to minor regulatory offenses where proof of a state of mind would be practically impossible; see *mens rea*

summation   See *closing argument*

Supremacy Clause   A clause in the federal Constitution that establishes the Constitution itself, treaties, and laws of congress to be the "supreme law of the land" to which all other laws must conform; see *federalism*

trial   A judicial examination and decision of a dispute between parties

trial jury   In criminal law, a jury consisting of 12 (or in some states six) individuals who attend a trial and render a verdict based on the law and the evidence

vacation of judgment   An appellate court's setting aside of a trial court's decision because of mistake or some other reason

verdict   "True declaration"; a trial jury's formal decision as to the facts of the case before it

voir dire   "To speak the truth"; the initial examination of potential jurors by a trial judge, the prosecutor, and the defense to determine their suitability to serve on a trial jury

wergild   "Man price"; in Germanic law, a sum paid by a wrongdoer to compensate a victim, or his or her lord or next of kin, for an injury

witness testimony   Statements of a witness at a grand jury hearing, trial, or some other court proceeding that serve as evidence

writ   A judicial order authorizing or requiring a person to do or refrain from doing a certain act

Bibliography

Bergman, Paul. *Trial Advocacy in a Nutshell*. St. Paul, Minn.: West Publishing Co., 1979.

Branham, Lynn S. *The Law and Policy of Sentencing and Corrections in a Nutshell*. 7th ed. St. Paul, Minn.: Thomson/West, 2005.

Cammack, Mark E. *Advanced Criminal Procedure in a Nutshell*. 2d ed. St. Paul, Minn.: Thomson/West, 2006.

Carp, Robert A., Ronald Stidham, and Kenneth L. Manning. *Judicial Process in America*. 7th ed. Washington, D.C.: CQ Press, 2007.

Clement, Mary J. *The Juvenile Justice System: Law and Process*. 2d ed. Boston: Butterworth-Heinemann, 2002.

Davies, Jack. *Legislative Law and Process in a Nutshell*. 2d ed. St. Paul, Minn.: West Publishing Co., 1986.

Delsohn, Gary. *The Prosecutors: A Year in the Life of a District Attorney's Office*. New York: Dutton Adult, 2003.

Feld, Barry C. *Juvenile Justice Administration in a Nutshell*. St. Paul, Minn.: West Group, 2003.

Graham, Michael H. *Federal Rules of Evidence in a Nutshell*. 7th ed. St. Paul, Minn.: Thomson/West, 2007.

Hickey, Thomas. *Taking Sides: Clashing Views in Crime and Criminology*. 8th ed. Dubuque, Iowa: McGraw-Hill/Dushkin, 2007.

Kerper, Hazel B. *Introduction to the Criminal Justice System*. 2d ed. St. Paul, Minn.: West Publishing Co., 1979.

LaFave, Wayne R., and Jerold H. Israel. *Criminal Procedure—Constitutional Limitations in a Nutshell*. 7th ed. St. Paul, Minn.: West Group, 2006.

LaFave, Wayne R. *Criminal Law*. 4th ed. St. Paul, Minn.: West Group, 2003.

LaFave, Wayne R., Jerold H. Israel, and Nancy J. King. *Criminal Procedure*. 3d ed. St. Paul, Minn.: West Group, 2000.

Langbein, John H. *The Origins of Adversary Criminal Trial*. New York: Oxford University Press, 2005.

Leo, Richard A. *Police Interrogation and American Justice*. Cambridge, Mass.: Harvard University Press, 2008.

Levi, Edward H. *An Introduction to Legal Reasoning*. Revised ed. Chicago: University of Chicago Press, 1962.

Levy, Leonard W. *Origins of the Bill of Rights*. New Haven, Conn.: Yale University Press, 2001.

Levy, Leonard W. *Origins of the Fifth Amendment: The Right Against Self-Incrimination*. New York: Oxford University Press, 1968.

Levy, Leonard W. *The Palladium of Justice: Origins of Trial by Jury*. Chicago: Ivan R. Dee, 1999.

Lewis, Anthony. *Gideon's Trumpet*. New York: Random House, 1964.

Loewy, Arnold H. *Criminal Law in a Nutshell*. 4th ed. St. Paul, Minn.: Thomson/West, 2003.

Molo, Steven F., and James R. Figliulo, eds. *Your Witness: Lessons on Cross-Examination*. Chicago: Law Bulletin Publishing Co., 2008.

Neubauer, David W. *America's Courts and the Criminal Justice System*. 9th ed. Belmont, Calif.: Wadsworth Publishing, 2007.

Oleszek, Walter J. *Congressional Procedures and the Policy Process*. 6th ed. Washington, D.C.: CQ Press, 2004.

Rosenthal, Alan. *The Third House: Lobbyists and Lobbying in the States*. Washington, D.C.: CQ Press, 2001.

Rothstein, Paul F., Myrna S. Raeder, and David Crump. *Evidence in a Nutshell*. 4th ed. St. Paul, Minn.: West Group Publishing, 2003.

Ryder, R. Scott, and Preston Elrod. *Juvenile Justice: A Social, Historical, and Legal Perspective*. 2d ed. Boston: Jones and Bartlett Publishers, 2005.

Schwartz, Bernard. *A History of the Supreme Court*. New York: Oxford University Press, 1995.

Smith, Christopher E., and George F. Cole. *Criminal Justice in America*. 5th ed. Belmont, Calif.: Wadsworth Publishing, 2007.

Walker, Samuel. *Popular Justice: A History of American Criminal Justice*. 2d ed. New York: Oxford University Press, 1997.

Whitebread, Charles H., and Christopher Slobogin. *Criminal Procedure: An Analysis of Cases and Concepts*. 4th ed. New York: Foundation Press, 2000.

Whitman, James Q. *The Origins of Reasonable Doubt: Theological Roots of the Criminal Trial*. New Haven, Conn.: Yale University Press, 2008.

Further Resources

Books

Alderman, Ellen, and Caroline Kennedy. *In Our Defense: The Bill of Rights in Action.* New York: HarperCollins, 1991.

> *Explores most of the criminal procedure provisions of the Bill of Rights (as well as noncriminal clauses) by examining real cases involving the interpretation of these rights.*

Bogira, Steve. *Courtroom 302: A Year Behind the Scenes in an American Criminal Courthouse.* New York: Vintage Books, 2006.

> *A gritty look at the real world of the criminal justice system, stripped of the romantic details that often appear in Hollywood television shows and films.*

Hickey, Thomas, and Gene Straughan. *Taking Sides: Clashing Views on Controversial Issues in Criminal Justice.* Dubuque, Iowa: McGraw-Hill/Dushkin, 2005.

> *Explores "pro" and "con" arguments in many areas of criminal procedure (both the investigation and trial phases) as well as other important stages of the criminal justice system.*

Multimedia

Anatomy of a Murder (1959), Columbia, 160 minutes, available on DVD.

> *An intense criminal drama, directed by Otto Preminger, that blends the technical side of the law with the personal motivations of those involved. Starring James Stewart.*

Irons, Peter, ed. *May It Please the Court: Live Recordings and Transcripts of Landmark Oral Arguments Made Before the Supreme Court Since 1955.* New York: New Press, 2007.

> *A trailblazing use of actual audio recordings of Supreme Court arguments, including some of the most famous criminal cases of the past half-century.*

To Kill a Mockingbird (1962), Universal, 129 minutes, available on DVD.

> *Starring Gregory Peck, one of the greatest of courtroom dramas, which also includes the racial and cultural background of a case that divides a small southern town, as seen through the eyes of young Scout Finch, the defense attorney's daughter.*

Witness for the Prosecution (1957), United Artists/MGM, 116 minutes, available on DVD.

A dramatized criminal trial, directed by Billy Wilder, that showcases the art of examination and cross-examination by one of England's greatest actors, Charles Laughton.

Web Sites

The Avalon Project

http://avalon.law.yale.edu/default.asp

A project of the Yale law School that contains a huge number of full-text sources dealing with law and legal history, including criminal law and procedure.

The Founders' Constitution

http://press-pubs.uchicago.edu/founders/

A clause-by-clause reference work that reprints documents comprising the background of each constitutional provision through the 12th Amendment, including the criminal law and procedure provisions of the original Constitution and the Bill of Rights.

How Our Laws Are Made / Enactment of a Law

http://thomas.loc.gov/home/lawsmade.toc.html
http://thomas.loc.gov/home/enactment/enactlawtoc.html

These pages, based on the Library of Congress website, detail the process of legislation at the federal level.

The Legal Information Institute at Cornell Law School

http://www.law.cornell.edu/

Contains texts and links of major sources of American law as well as surveys of criminal law, criminal procedure, and more specific criminal topics.

Sourcebook of Criminal Justice Statistics

http://www.albany.edu/sourcebook/

A site containing links to a wealth of information on every aspect of criminal justice.

Index

About the Author

Buckner F. Melton, Jr. holds a doctorate in history from Duke University and a law degree from the University of North Carolina at Chapel Hill. He specializes in areas of national security history, including impeachment, treason, and constitutional war powers. His book *The First Impeachment: The Constitution's Framers and the Case of Senator William Blount* received national attention during the impeachment proceedings against President Clinton. During the impeachment Melton served as an advisor to several members of Congress and as a commentator for National Public Radio, *NewsHour* with Jim Lehrer, and MSNBC. He is also the author of *Aaron Burr: Conspiracy to Treason*, *A Hanging Offense: The Strange Affair of the Warship* Somers, and *Sea Cobra: Admiral Halsey's Task Force and the Great Pacific Typhoon*. He currently serves as Distinguished Writer-in-Residence and University Press Fellow at Mercer University.